Gone But Not Forgotten

A
PHOTO-HISTORY
1904-1967

By

Chuck Wlodarczyk

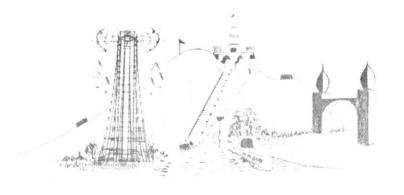

RIVERVIEW PUBLICATIONS
745 Goodwin Drive
Park Ridge, Illinois 60068

First Printing August 1977
Second Printing November 1977
Third Printing September 1978
Fourth Printing July 1979
Fifth Printing April 1980
Sixth Printing March 1981
Seventh Printing October 1984
Eighth Printing November 1986
Ninth Printing November 1987
Tenth Printing October 1989
Eleventh Printing June 1992
Twelfth Printing September 1993
Thirteenth Printing July 1996
Fourteenth Printing February 1998
Fifteenth Printing January 2001

Library of Congress Catalog Card Number 77-082595
ISBN 0-911694-07-2

Acknowledgements

I wish to express my gratitude to the following people for their contributions, whether they were photographs, memories, statistics, or just plain time, energy and patience (especially on the part of my family). Thank you again . . .

LEROY DAUNIS
FRANK FOURNIER
ED FRANK, JR.
ROBERT GARCIA
TED KELLER
GARY KIPNIS
JOHN KOLBERG
MURPHY LONG
JOHN LUKA
MARTY and FRAN MEYER
RAY NICHOLS
NORM OYEN
GEORGE PRITZEN
BILL REFFKE
KEN REIGER
CHUCK SCHADEN
CHUCK SIMZYK
WALTER SMITH
DOROTHY and JOE TEMPLIN
ENGEL THORSTENSEN

A special thanks to the Chicago Sun Times

Dedication

Dedicated to my Wife

"Jan"

Who was such a great help in putting

this book together . . .

And to all Riverview Fans

Wherever they may be.

Comments on Author

I would like to mention the fact that I in no way claim to be an expert on Riverview. By this I mean that much of the information and facts I have given in the book were supplied to me by former employees of Riverview, Leroy Daunis, who worked for the park for some 25 years, and Chuck Simzyk, who was the Purchasing Agent for 32 years. So with the years of head knowledge that these men have and the photographs that I either took myself or collected over the years, I have become a super Riverview buff. This book has been in my dreams for several years, and I hope to share some pictures and information you'll find interesting.

I have been asked numerous questions by *The Chicago Tribune's* "Action Line" column and also by *The Chicago Sun Times' "Action Time"* column to help out their readers whose interest in Riverview continues. I have also presented numerous Riverview talks and slide shows in the Chicagoland area since the park's closing in 1967. I have also appeared on several radio talk shows.

As a native Chicagoan, living in Wyoming for 12 years, I loved Riverview and never really thought there would be a time that it would not exist. But here we are today, No Riverview. I've traveled around the country and ride coasters whenever I can, so maybe I'll meet you on one in the future.

I do not want to get into rating roller coasters here, I do have a top 10 or 15 list, but there are so many great coasters thru out the U.S. that I'll leave the ratings up to others. My ALL TIME favorite coaster, the grand-daddy of them all was "THE BOBS" at Riverview. If you wish to try a few of the current great coaster rides try these: the Texas Cyclone - Astroworld, Houston, Texas, the Thunderbolt - Kennywood Park, West Mifflin, Pennsylvania, Mr. Twister - Elitch's Gardens, Denver, Colorado, the Cyclone - Lakeside Park, Denver, Colorado, the Colossus - Magic Mountain, Valencia, California, the American Eagle - Great America, Gurnee, Illinois, the Roaring Tiger - Circus World, Haines City, Florida, the Cyclone - Coney Island, New York, Swamp Fox - Myrtle Beach, South Carolina, Thunderroad - Charlotte, North Carolina area, Wildcat - Idora Park, Youngstown, Ohio, Giant Dipper - Santa Cruz, California, Giant Coaster - Dorney Park, Allentown, Pennsylvania, Cyclone - Riverside Park, Agawam, Massachusetts, Tornado - Adventureland Park, Des Moines, Iowa area, The Beast and the Racer - Kings Island, Cincinatti, Ohio, Judge Roy Scream - Six Flags Over Texas, Arlington, Texas, Screaming Eagle - Six Flags Over Mid-America, St. Louis, Missouri, The Great American Scream Machine - Six Flags Over Georgia, Atlanta, Georgia, the Comet - Crystal Beach, Ontario, Canada, Rolling Thunder - Great Adventure, Jackson, New Jersey, Zingo - Bell's Amusement Park, Tulsa, Oklahoma, The Grizzly and Rebel Yell - King's Dominion, Doswell, Virginia, Zippin Pippin - Libertyland, Memphis, Tennessee.

These are just a few of the great coasters that will give you thrills and chills and the euphoria of negative and positive G's as well as some great curves and ups and downs. So KEEP ON COASTIN!!!

— Chuck Wlodarczyk

FOREWORD

Riverview is gone, but not forgotten, at least I know I'll never forget it . . . .

Being a native of Chicago and growing up within a mile of Riverview, I realized at a young age, as all children did back then, that Riverview was a maze of wonders, noises and delicious popcorn and cotton candy smells. No other place in Chicago could compare to the great Riverview.

I was about six years old when I made my first visit to the park. Since we lived so close, we walked. From blocks away we could see looming high in the sky the Pair-O-Chutes tower. Getting closer, I could hear the clanking of the chains that pulled the roller coasters up the high hills. I could also hear the screams of the people as they plunged down the hills of the coasters.

We made it to the main gate and passed through the turnstyle. Even at my young age you could not help but admit that the gate and the park was old but still massively beautiful.

The war years were on then, so the Banjo Light fixtures found throughout the park, (which came from the World's Fair), were blaring military march songs. I was tired after the walk to the park, but once inside I was in a hurry to look around and go walk the 2½ mile midway and ride as many rides as I could. It was an experience I'll never forget. My first roller coaster ride back then was on the "wicked and wild Greyhound." Well, it seemed that wild to me at that age. That only began my desire for bigger and faster roller coasters.

At about 10 or 11 years old, I finally built up enough courage to take on the daddy of all roller coasters, "the Bobs." To this day the Bobs was the roughest, fastest coaster I have ever been on. It seems from my early experiences riding coasters, I have become addicted. I'm now a roller coaster addict, looking to ride them whenever I go on vacation. The wooden type (actually the Bobs type) coasters are getting harder to find, but if they are near where I'm going, I'll try to find the time to ride at least once.

Thanks to my Uncle, a photographer, I got interested in photography. Thus my trips to Riverview began to have twofold purposes; one to enjoy the rides, and secondly to photograph them. Going to the park during the days and also evenings were important so that some of the grandiose scenes of the park could be captured on film.

I was shocked and saddened, when the announcement was made after the closing of the 1967 season, that Riverview was to be permanently closed. It's 2¢ days and 5¢ nights will be remembered by Chicagoans for a long time. You just can't forget 64 years of a park billed as the "World's Largest Amusement Park."

I have put this book together because of the interest so many people have expressed in Riverview. I hope you'll find the text enjoyable and interesting and the photographs should speak for themselves. It is my sincere desire to help you relive the fun times you had at Riverview remembering its motto often heard on radio and T.V., "laugh your troubles away at Riverview."

Go with me now with words and pictures through the years of 1904-1967, because Riverview may be gone, but truly is not forgotten . . . .

Chuck Wlodarczyk

This aerial view shows the boundaries of Riverview and if you look closely you'll be able to see and pick out some of the rides; note the park's seven roller coasters. (L. Daunis)

Remember seeing this sign on Western Avenue announcing the final season's opening date in 1967. (L. Daunis)

On Addison Street you were reminded of the Mardi Gras Parade in 1966. (L. Daunis)

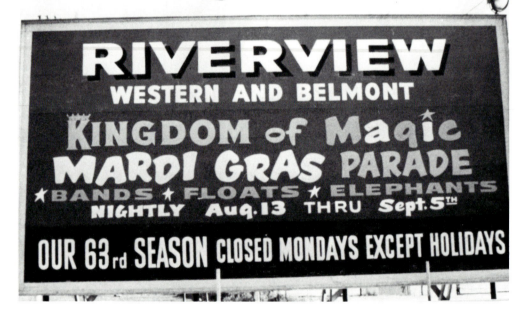

Did you ever park in lot adjacent to Lane Tech High School? This is where you went in if you did. (L. Daunis)

RIVERVIEW—Gone But Not Forgotten

Millions came to "Riverview" and millions left having had a great time there. Located on Chicago's northwest side, the official mailing address was 3300 N. Western Avenue, but to all Riverview lovers that address meant the main gate. The "world's largest amusement park" was bounded on the East by Western Avenue, on the West

The red, white and blue main entrance was recognized by all. (J. Luka)

Maybe you will recall this older view of the main entrance. (J. Kolberg)

by the Chicago River, the South boundary was Belmont Avenue and Lane Tech High School was the North boundary.

Each year 3 million or more people in the Chicagoland area received free entrance passes through the mail. During the 1920's another bargain was enjoyed by kids. The park paid the streetcar fare to and from the park for kids. Of course, the fare back there was only about 2¢, but in those days that meant a great deal to people.

SPECIAL BARGAINS OFTEN

Bargains were not unusual at Riverview, since the rides were so reasonably priced. The most expensive ride, probably one of the most popular, was the Bobs. Prices ranged from 25¢ to 50¢ for the first ride and about 20¢ to 35¢ for second rides. The cheapest rides, only in price that is, were the Tilt-A-Whirl at 5¢ to 10¢, the Caterpillar and Greyhound also fell into this category. For example, these rides were 2¢ and 5¢ on 2¢ and 5¢ nights. The same applied to the miniature train rides. Based on the reasonableness of the prices at Riverview, a person young or old, could go on each and every ride two or three times and spend no more than $10.00 or $15.00. Of course, you would have to add a few more dollars if you played any of many games that dotted the park.

All types of games could be found at Riverview: Guess your Age or Weight (if you were brave enough to let others know), rifle ranges, horse race game, the rabbit race game. There was the fishing pond where every player was a winner. For basketball players, the Basketball Toss was intriguing. People always played the coke bottle game. Remember a favorite of all was "Skee Ball." This game is still found in almost every amusement park. Were you fascinated by Fascination? Maybe your favorite was the African Dip. The nail game looked so easy that young men would try to show their strength by driving the nails with only three swings into the tree stump. They soon found out it seemed to be made of lead. If these didn't seem to be enough, you could have played bingo for prizes rather than money, at Stop and Shop. You could have always visited the Penny Arcade where pinball machines of all sorts could be found.

Do you remember Pop-Eye or the Tattooed Lady? If you do, then you must remember the Palace of Wonders, or more commonly known as the Freak Show. Another side show to attract you was the Motorcycle Syndrome. In this show, men would ride their cycles on the walls. ON THE WALLS??? that's right, I know that sounds strange, but I saw them do so. The riders in the Motorcycle Syndrome use to ask for money from the people before and after the show. The riders claimed that because the riding stunts were so dangerous, they could not get any insurance. If everyone gave them even small change, they told the people that it would help them if any accidents happened during the show. I'm not sure if they had insurance or not, but I do know the small change really mounted up to big dollars.

JOIN IN A WORD AND PHOTO TOUR

Do you remember these things? I'm sure you do, so why not join me in a 2½ mile word and photo tour of "Riverview, The World's Largest Amusement Park."

Just inside the main gate we could not help admiring one of the beautiful flower gardens found in the park. Lifting our eyes, we could see the Tilt-A-Whirl ride.

Just inside the main gate you saw this beautiful flower garden and you were welcomed by the sign showing the "Bargain Days." The Flash tracks are in the background.
(L. Daunis)

If you look real closely you may be able to pick yourself out of the crowd.
(C. Wlodarczyk)

10

This building being so ornate was the big difference between Riverview's Tilt-A-Whirl and others found today. (J. Kolberg, collection of K. Reiger)

Housed in an ornate structure, the ride might have been placed strategically in this location to condition our stomachs for other rides that day. Actually the Tilt-A-Whirl, outside of the structure covering it and its age, was not much different from the ones found at summer carnivals or fairs.

To the right of the flower garden, we could always find out what new rides or attractions the park offered that season, because this was where the welcome sign was located. If we had just gotten off the Tilt-A-Whirl we would more than likely be a little dizzy. But with wobbly legs, we head over to bigger and better things.

The Silver Flash, a gleaming shrouded covered monster that climbed ever so slowly up that first hill. For 20¢ to 35¢ you could reach the top of that 65 foot hill and down and up the rest of the hills, giving you a thrill of thrills. Maybe the name "The Pippin" sounds more familiar to you or perhaps the Silver Streak, Silver Flash or lastly the Flash might be more recognizable. These were the names this ride had over the years. In the 1930's, when the ride was called the Pippin, some cars of the train uncoupled and collided, injuring over 60 people. To help people forget this tragedy, the name was changed to the Silver Streak and new cars were bought. This name was changed sometime later to the Silver Flash. The final name "The Flash" was given the ride after the entrance was remodeled. The Flash was certainly a ride worth enjoying.

Get your pennies and nickels ready you are about to enter the biggest Penny Arcade in the park. It was located just west of the Flash. This arcade had a wide variety of 1¢ to 5¢ games. Remember the Steam Shovel game. There was a watch

11

Close-up view of the welcome sign shows the announcement of Mardi Gras for 1967; but if it had been taken in the early season you would have seen what new ride opened that season. (L. Daunis)

The clanking chains carrying the shrouded Silver Flash train up its first hill. (C. Wlodarczyk)

This is what the Flash looked like from the front when it was standing in the loading platform.

almost always in the sand and you would try to get the shovel's claws to pick it up. I always came up with a lot of sand or maybe a marble, how about you? Many people enjoyed putting pennies in the post card machines, they received movie star cards, comic cards and, of course, post cards of Riverview.

LET'S GO STROLLING DOWN THE MIDWAY

Proceeding down the midway, on our left we come upon The Wild Mouse. Previously on this site were the twin Ferris wheels that thousands rode and enjoyed. These were side by side Ferris wheels. Getting back, though, to the steel coaster that was a terror to all who rode it: The Mouse cars zipped around on two steel rails, making 45 degree turns. On these turns, you were certain that you were going to go over the side, especially when you saw the front of the car going straight when the tracks turned. Just in the nick of time however, we were saved, the car would abruptly turn, dip you down some speedy hills and bring you into the platform safely.

Putting our feet on solid ground again was shortlived, across the midway, behold a roller coaster, originally called the Sky Rocket and known later as the Blue Streak. These cars were shrouded similarly to the Silver Flash, only these trains were

13

Looking down the midway in 1956 you could see the twin Ferris Wheels, the Blue Streak entrance, the Dodgem ticket booth and the Flash tracks in the background. (C. Wlodarczyk

The tall tracks shown belong to the Fireball, but the lower tracks were the steel tracks of the Wild Mouse. In the foreground is one of Riverviews gardens, also you see the pond for the Showboat ride. (C. Wlodarczyk)

14

The Blue Streak entrance and tracks in 1942. (L. Daunis)

painted blue. To roller coaster buffs, the first hill left a little to be desired. It had a double dip rather than a steep drop off. Since this coaster was not one of the more popular ones and also to relieve some of the crowded lines on the Bobs the Fireball was built.

The original idea for the new Fireball was to have the first hill 100 feet high or 15 feet higher than the Bobs' first hill. City ordinances restricted the construction of a hill this high. What the park did to get around this ordinance and yet be legal, was to take out the double dip hill of the Blue Streak, then by digging into the ground and rebuilding the first hill, the Fireball achieved second place in the roller coaster popularity at the park. The new Fireball tracks were placed 10 feet into the ground, but the Bobs still held the record in the first hill height.

With the reconstruction on the Fireball, speed was certainly added. Advertising campaigns made claims that the Fireball was Riverview's fastest coaster, hitting record speeds of 100 MPH, but it was really more like 65 MPH. New open-top cars were installed, painted a bright red. On the main entrance to this ride a giant red fireball head was installed and of course, that which goes with remodeling, new pricing. To ride the Fireball 25¢ to 40¢ was needed, still a reasonable price for fun. Check the illustration of the tracks and roller coaster cars, showing the revamping of the tracks for the Fireball for a more detailed look.

15

The #1 Blue Streak train
going down the second dip
on the first hill. It was
located right over the loading
platform. (L. Daunis)

Continuing our day of fun, we come to the building housing another popular favorite. Here driving cars and colliding with others was quite legal, in fact it was the only way to have fun. It may have seemed to be a little stuffy but as on all the rides, rules had to be followed. The Dodgem operators were always yelling the instructions for the drivers to follow, "Move in a counter clockwise direction." The reason for this was to avoid jam-ups. You collided and hit other cars as long as you remained in a counter clockwise flow. The Dodgem or as it was called later, the Bump-em, was popular with young as well as oldsters. I think everyone enjoyed taking their frustrations out by smashing into other cars, I know I did.

Hidden partially in cloud of black smoke was the next for us to see and ride. The little steam locomotives till 1948 were called the Red Devil and the Blue Devil. Both pulled passengers in little wooden coaches. This was a long ride that started and

One of Riverview's bargain rides — only 5c to ride again. Notice the man in the foreground releasing the brakes and the other man collecting second ride fares. Remember lining up on the Blue Streak like the people in the picture? (L. Daunis)

17

The crew in 1943 on the
Blue Streak Roller coaster.
Do those jumpsuits look
familiar? (L. Daunis)

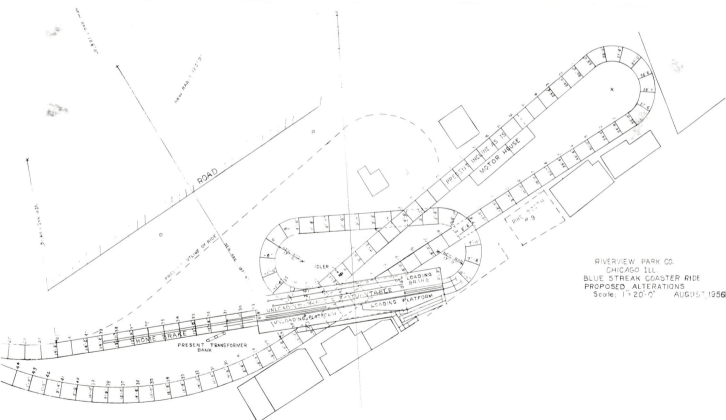

This original blue print shows the modification of the first hill elevations
from the old Blue Streak to the new Fireball roller coaster. (L. Daunis)

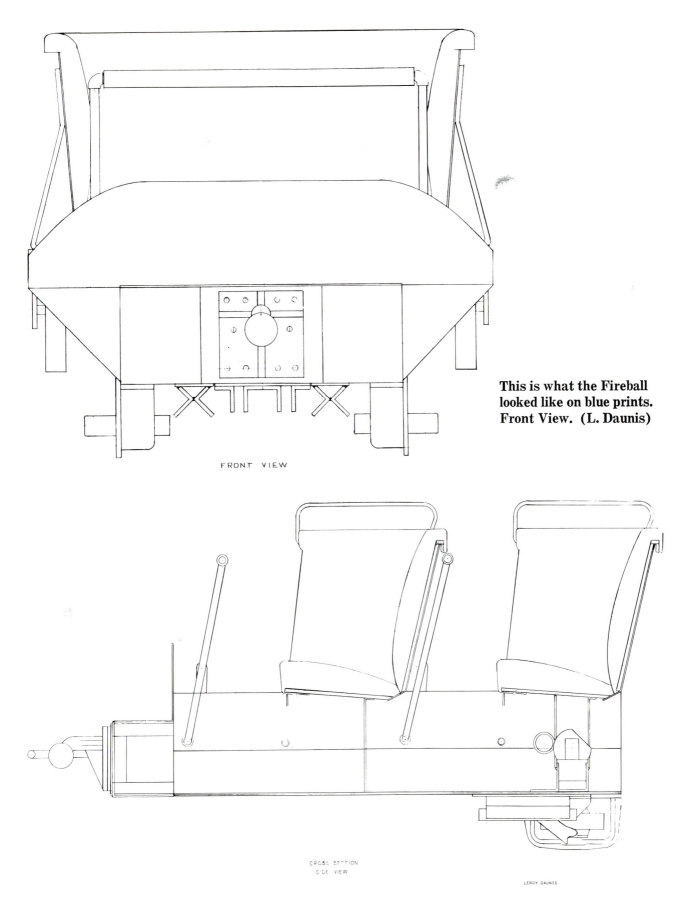

FRONT VIEW

This is what the Fireball
looked like on blue prints.
Front View. (L. Daunis)

CROSS SECTION
SIDE VIEW

LEROY DAUNIS

FIREBALL CAR
SCALE; $\frac{1}{4}$"=1"   MAY 27, 1959

Sideview of the Fireball cars in blue print. (L. Daunis)

In this photo notice the Fireball heads on the Cashier's cage and the large one on the loading platform. (L. Daunis)

The Fireball flashes down the first hill to the delights or frights of the riders. (C. Wlodarczyk)

Can you hear the screams of the people on the Fireball coaster as they descend the first hill?
(C. Wlodarczyk)

The old Dodgem had a new paint job, new name and new cars for the final few seasons. (L. Daunis)

Diesel Streamliners, Riverview Chief and Riverview Scout wait to load passengers. Note atomic energy building in background.

ended across from the freak show and Caterpillar ride. In 1948 the steam engines were replaced with streamliners or diesel locomotives. These were named the Riverview Scout which was colored green, black and yellow, and the Riverview Chief which was black, red and yellow. The trains took us on a relaxing trip around the inside of the park. Just relax and enjoy the sights.

Heading toward the Caterpillar, we heard the barker from the Palace of Wonders calling out to come and see the show. Remember the Hoochie-Koochie dancers drawing the crowds. Maybe Pop-Eye was out in front doing his trick. Many were drawn inside to see the Tattooed Lady, the Tallest Man, the Smallest Man, the Fat Lady, the Rubber Man and the list went on and on.

The Caterpillar was an old ride, it whirled you around, while being covered by a canvas hood. The Caterpillar had gentle dips and on a hot day or evening it would cool you off. Moneywise, the Caterpillar was one of the economical rides—15¢ on the

Pop-Eye does his thing outside the Palace of Wonders or freak show. (L. Daunis)

average and sometimes free, if you could get a guest ticket. Leaving this ride we might decide to stop and take a refreshment break. The Palm Gardens, Casino or Beer Gardens (just a few of its many names) had much to offer. While sitting and watching people you might have had a soda or maybe beer with your hot dog. Delicious wasn't it?

23

The barker shouts "Step right up folks and see what's inside." Guess what year this was taken? Maybe the clothes will give the date away. (C. Simzyk)

In the off season this is what the midway looked like. Notice the Caterpillar in the foreground and the miniature golf course across the way. (L. Daunis)

After resting a bit, we move across the main walkway where you could see the Dancing Waters or the Life Show or as it was called in its last few seasons the Safari Ride. This was nothing more than cars riding through dark tunnels with various creatures lighting up and popping out at you. Lighting and sound effects gave you some thrills on this ride.

ROMANTIC RIDE THROUGH TUNNEL OF LOVE

After adjusting our eyes to either bright sun or lights we move on to the 1000 Islands ride. You don't recognize that name? How about Mill on the Floss or Tunnel of Love or its last name the Old Mill. When this ride was called the 1000 Islands it had only the boats or canoes and canals and no tunnels. Later when the name was changed, the tunnels were built. I guess the best name for this ride was the Tunnel of Love; you could always see couples of all ages including sailors and their dates going on this ride, through the tunnels and along the nicely landscaped canals. They said they were enjoying the relaxing ride, who was I to question them? After the tunnels were once installed, the only change made to the ride was the front entrance. It might have been rebuilt or just repainted, whatever would be needed to resemble the new name. For example, when it was called the Tunnel of Love, hearts were painted on the front; when the ride was called the Old Mill, the front was changed to resemble an old wooden mill.

Remember if you can, when you got off the Tunnel of Love, another water ride was located right across the midway. The lines were always long for this ride. In fact, waiting made the ride seem like more fun, anticipation added to the excitement. The ride everyone recognized, and enjoyed by all, was called Shoot the Chutes. The lines led us to brightly colored boats, entering the boats we rode down a narrow man-made canal into a long dark tunnel. Before reaching the tunnel we heard a recorded

Can you pick out yourself in this 1948 photo? Young and old enjoyed the Mill on the Floss boat ride. It was later known as Tunnel of Love, (John Kolberg)

Around 1910 you could have been in one of these boats on the 1000 Island ride. Surrounding the ride you can see the Velvet Coaster.

The Old Mill was the final of 4 names for the ride shown here in early 1967. Other names were 1000 Islands, Mill on the Floss and the Tunnel of Love.
(L. Daunis)

message "Keep your arms and hands inside the boat. Please remain seated and do not rock the boat." If you don't remember hearing that, you probably remember seeing signs that said similar things on every ride. Remember some of them: "Caution, Don't Stand Up, Remove your eyeglasses while riding this device. Only 2 people to a seat, Remain seated while ride is in motion, etc."

Getting back, however, to the Chutes ride, we are about to enter the tunnel, reaching the end of the tunnel there was an elevator used to take us up to the top of the Chutes tower. On the ride up to the top, the slowly climbing elevator afforded us a beautiful view of the park. Reaching the top, we feel a slight jerk. Pausing momentarily, we get to see what we are about to experience. From our viewpoint we can see the slide, we can also see the huge and seemingly deep splash pond. I say seemingly deep, because at the base of the hill and slide, the merky water was only 4½ feet deep, shallowing down to about 18 inches deep at the far end of the pond. Dipping forward suddenly, the boat leaves the tower, racing downhill towards the splash pond. In just a few seconds we are bouncing up and down on the water, catching sprays of water on our faces. Did you ever wonder how the boat operator kept his balance in the back of the boat without falling overboard, when here we were holding on for dear life? It took some practice runs I'm sure. As the boat operator steered the boat to shore, the man in the white jumpsuit would use a long-handled hook to bring us close to land so that we could get out and dry off. A ride on the Shoot the Chutes was really worth the 25¢ to 40¢ charge.

While drying off we looked around for our next adventure. If we had small children with us, we would have to make sure and stop at Kiddyland #1 or as some

From the Space Ride looking back toward the main gate you can see some of the many concessions that were spread throughout the park. (J. Kolberg)

I was riding the Space Ride when I shot this view, you can see the Chutes Tower and pond, the Paratrooper in the background also the Comet roller coaster entrance and the Chutes Kiddyland or Kiddyland #1. (C. Wlodarczyk)

27

A good view of the Chutes Tower and giant slide, you'll also see the canal leading to the tunnel that took you to the elevator for your ride to the top. (C. Wlodarczyk)

One of the Chutes boats hitting the pond at the base of the slide. (J. Kolberg)

Another Chutes boat hits the water splashing water on its riders. (C. Wlodarczyk)

Ground level view of a Chutes boat hitting the pond at the deep end (4½ feet deep). Notice the second ride price 15c. (J. Kolberg)

Remember all those people telling you how deep the water in the pond was, well don't believe them; now you have proof. It was only 4 to 5 feet at the base of the slide and at the shallow end only about 18 inches. (J. Luka)

Riverview's beauty truly is shown in this shot taken at dusk. (C. Wlodarczyk)

A wave of white churning water is left in the wake of this boat. (J. Kolberg)

The Chutes Tower at Nite. (C. Wlodarczyk)

called it The Chutes Kiddyland. The kids would go bananas in Kiddyland, the ride assortment ranged from little cars and boats to a small whip, a miniature tumble bug, a small carousel and a little turtle ride. Not very exciting to adults, but to kids it was great.

Across the way from the Kiddyland #1 area was the Big Whip. It ran on a long oval track, slowly at first; that is, until you reached the corners. Here is where the name came from, at the corners you were whipped around a 90 degree curve. For 10¢ to 20¢ you could enjoy a ride on the Whip.

Right next to the Big Whip was the northwest platform of the Space Ride. The Space Ride was installed at Riverview for a cost of $375,000.00. That doesn't sound

Looks like the Kiddyland #1 Whip had quite a few riders. You can see the picnic grove in the background and of course the ever-famous Pair-O-Chutes Tower. (J. Kolberg)

like so much for this type of ride, but back in 1963 that was quite high. Rides like the Space Ride are found throughout the country in different amusement parks. You could board the Space Ride car between the Whip and the Comet roller coaster in the northwest corner of the park and glide over the cables to the southeast corner between the Ghost Train ride and Aladdin's Castle Fun House. The fares back in 1963 were 35¢ for a one way ride and 50¢ for a round trip fare. The prices were reduced later as the Space Ride was not one of the more popular rides. Many of the

A band playing during the Charlie Weber Day, marching past the Big Whip. In the background you can see the Hades fun house. (B. Reffke)

The Space Ride cars coming and going from the Northwest platform of the ride's entrance. This platform was right between the Whip and the Comet. (C. Wlodarczyk)

Top left — At the foot of the Chutes Tower you could find the tea-cup ride called the Cuddle-Up but as the picture shows the name was changed to the Crazy Dazy. (L. Daunis)

Top right — This photo taken in 1940 shows the old Zephyr that later became known as the Comet. (W. Smith)

Left — Hades only had this paint job for a few years because, as you can see, it required a great deal of detail and work. (M. Long)

photographs appearing in the book were taken from the Space Ride. This ride offered a grand aerial view of the other rides in the park. Shortly after the ride opened, I was fortunate to ride on one of the few cars that were not screened, so the photographs taken had no obstructions to detract from the park's beauty. Unfortunately the cars had to be screened in because people, being what they are, could not control themselves. They would throw junk on the people and the rides below. During the four years the Space Ride operated at Riverview, even with the reduced fares, the ride did not pay for itself.

Taking a round-trip ride on the Space Ride we would get off ready to spin our stomachs on the Cuddle-Up or known as the Crazy Dazy when the park closed. This cup and saucer type ride spun you around making figure eights for only 15¢ to 25¢. An exciting cheapie ride!

Dizzily walking across the midway we come to the Comet roller coaster. The Comet trains were covered and similar looking to the Silver Flash and the Blue Streak but the Comet was a little bit rougher. Also different from the previous coasters was the fact that this coaster began by going through a tunnel and then up the first hill then around and down. Riding the last seat of the last car, my favorite of course, lifted you right out of the seat going downhill and slammed you against the seat again as you climbed the next hill. A good ride, previously called the Big Dipper and then the Zephyr.

It is at this point that we reach the riverwalk portion of the park; at this bend in the midway, we would find the Paratrooper ride. The Paratrooper was an umbrella type ride that ran at a 30 degree angle, you can find this ride at many carnivals and also at many amusement parks. Before the Paratrooper many will remember what was found on this spot. Do you recall the first fun house at Riverview? If you do then you remember Hades. Dark corridors, flashing figures and weird sounds were inside

This was taken while walking on riverwalk. From this angle you can see the elevator portion of the Chutes Tower, you get a good view of the Strat-O-Stat planes in motion and you can also see the Monkey Town or Jungle. The building in the foreground housed the Merry-Go-Round.
(C. Wlodarczyk)

Hades. The reason it had to be replaced was that the Chicago river was right behind Hades and the water was washing away the ground under the building, a good reason for replacing it, I would say.

Leaving Hades and continuing on riverwalk we note that we are behind the Chutes tower. Looking closely you can see the elevator we mentioned earlier, going up to the top of tower loaded with fun-seeking people.

In this night time (time exposure) shot, you can see the Chutes, Strat-O-Stat, Monkey Races and the Merry-Go-Round. (C. Wlodarczyk)

Monkey Town, Monkey Circus, Monkey Jungle were the various names of this game that you could play for 15c or 2 chances for 25c. (C. Simzyk)

Wonder what the streaks of light flashing by the Chutes Tower are? This is an action time exposure showing the Strat-O-Stat planes flying. (J. Kolberg)

Dolls were won at the Monkey Races; the big dolls in the 1940's, the little doll in the 1950's. At right is the Drum Major. Dolls owned by Engel Thorstensen. (C. Wlodarczyk)

Almost everyone who ever went to Riverview remembers the Monkey Races. The terrified little monkeys were so cute everyone would have liked to pet them, but the operators as well as signs warned that "Monkeys Do Bite." Did you ever place a bet on which monkey would win? For a quarter you could pick a certain colored car to stop on a number of your choice. If you picked the right color and number you'd win! The odds, of course were with the game, if only one person played, the odds were 19 to 1 that you would win. If 2, 3 or 4 cars were played, the odds were 76 to 4, that means 4 winners to 76 losers. Monkey Races, Monkey Town or Monkey Jungle was very descriptively named.

Next to the Monkey Races was one of the oldest rides in the park originally known as the Aero-O-Stat. When the park closed, the same ride with larger planes still occupied this spot, only you'll remember it like I do as the Stratostat. You could ride these planes that circled around its center tower picking up speed and height for 10 or 20¢.

People are soaring high in the Strat-O-Stat planes, while crowds gathered to see if their monkeys won. Look at all that wood in the Chutes Tower. (J. Kolberg)

The Strat-O-Stat plane glides by the Chutes slide. (J. Kolberg)

If we stayed at the
Beer Garden too long,
then by the time we
reached the Strat-O-Stat,
it might have looked
like this. Night photo.
(C. Wlodarczyk)

Next to the Stratostat stood the big Carousel or Merry-Go-Round. Big it was, with its 70 hand-carved horses and its four Lover's Chariots that were 11 feet high. The Merry-Go-Round was built by the Philadelphia Toboggan Company in 1906. It was one of the largest and most beautiful carousels ever built. The hand-carved horses are valued at around $2500.00 each today. You can see why Riverview was proud of it, so proud in fact, that they kept it in top notch shape. After the park closed, it was sold to the town of Galena, Illinois, only to be stored and never used. Later it was purchased by and is still operating at Six Flags over Georgia. The ride still carries the name "Riverview Carousel." For 15 pennies we could ride the Merry-Go-Round or, as it was once called, the Fairyland Ride.

The Merry-Go-Round undergoing extensive remodeling between the 1966 and 1967 season. (L. Daunis)

The Merry-Go-Round looked like this in the spring of 1967 after the remodeling was finished. Doesn't it look ready to serve the happy children? (L. Daunis)

These horses from the Merry-Go-Round are ready to prance. They're proud of their new paint job. (L. Daunis)

The 11 foot Lover's Chariots got a fresh coat of paint for the 1967 season. (L. Daunis)

40

Are you ready to ride another roller coaster? Technically the Flying Turns was only a combination roller coaster/bobsled type ride though. Rather than going up and down hills, you found yourself riding the sides of the walls in a half barrel structure. The ride cost 20 to 35 cents plus waiting time to ride. The ride itself was short, but the waiting lines were always long. This fun ride came from the World's Fair of the 1930's. The Flying Turns replaced a Kiddie Coaster called the Kiddie Bobs.

Walking parallel to the river in the foreground you can see the Flying Turns. In the background You can see the old Bobs entrance with its majestic columns. (C. Wlodarczyk)

INDIANAPOLIS 500 RACE CARS BEFORE 1948

If we had been walking down riverwalk prior to 1948 we would have now approached the Indianapolis 500 Racing Cars. This ride was composed of little gasoline powered cars. In 1948 this ride was replaced by the Bubble Bounce. On this ride there were square cars on a round table. The cars spun around and the table bounced up and down on a 45 degree tilt. The spinning could be controled by the riders as there was a wheel in each car. On this stomach-churning ride the operator told me that he was always cleaning up, if you know what I mean.

Next on riverwalk, Riverview's most famous roller coaster. The daddy of them all THE BOBS. The only thing peaceful and tranquil on the Bobs was the little flower garden in front of the entrance. Which entrance is more familiar to you, the Grecian Columns or the new $30,000.00 neon sign? Everyone has their own favorite choice, but mine was the columns. For 35¢ to 50¢ you would have the ride of your life and I do mean ride. Patience was always needed on the Bobs, because you always had to wait in line as it was so popular. While waiting you quickly realized that this ride was not

41

for the faint-hearted, just looking at the pale people getting off let you know that. Then look at the seats, all padded, huge safety bars, both only confirmed your previous assumption that this definitely was not a chicken ride.

Do you recognize the flower garden in front of the Bobs roller coaster? It was the only thing peaceful about the giant ride. (M. Long)

The BOBS

DID YOU EVER LOSE EARRINGS, HATS, ETC.?

Across from the loading platform were the warning signs about loose objects, eyeglasses, hats, etc. By the way, do you remember seeing the little crow's nest above the loading platform with a man sitting in it? The man in the crow's next was the ride controller, it was this man who determined when it was safe for the train to leave the platform and begin its ride. He also sounded just like a recorded message when he said "Let's ride again, 25¢, stand behind the red line till the train stops." Then he would very curtly say "load them up, two to a seat." On all the coasters you would see a crow's nest and the message was always the same, except for the second ride price.

The Bobs train consisted of 11 cars, each weighing 900 pounds empty. The first hill of the Bobs stood about 85 feet high with a steep drop. The Bobs really was a wicked ride! Riding in the front seat offered nothing more than seeing where you were going, as if you cared when you reached the top of hill number 1. I always waited for the last seat of the last car because the ride was best there. The ride was faster in the last seat because all the weight of the train pulled you down the hills, almost like a whip sensation. Actually in the first car you were at the bottom of the

As always, the Bobs #2 train loaded with riders climbs up the first 85-foot hill. (C. Wlodarczyk)

Plunging down the first crest is the #1 train of the Bobs. Now its hang on and brace yourselves for the oncoming sharp curves and steep hills. (C. Wlodarczyk)

The #2 train whips around the low front curve on riverwalk. This is about the only place where people would let go of the lap bar and raise their arms to onlookers. (C. Wlodarczyk)

44

The #1 train is whipping around the front curve and the #2 train is climbing the first hill. Notice the heavy rubber grip bars on both sides of the cars that were designed to be used to brace yourself on the curves. (J. Kolberg)

Another angle shot of the #1 Bobs train. The timing on the Bobs was precise so that
when 3 trains were being run they could leave the platform every 20 seconds. (J. Kolberg)

As the train rounds that curve, note how most of the people were slammed against the one side. My favorite entrance is shown in this shot, I liked the huge white columns. How about you?
(C. Wlodarczyk)

From this vantage point you could get an unobstructed view of the trains rounding the curve and climbing the first hill. This was actually the most photographed spot on the Bobs because of this.
(C. Wlodarczyk)

The new expensive sign for the Bobs is shown here. (L. Daunis)

hill before the train really picked up the speed you felt coming down that first hill in the last seat. WOW!!! What a fantastic ride. The trains had railroad type flanged wheels which allowed for the sharply banked curves.

The Bobs considered by many as the number one ride at Riverview, I know this is how I felt. The way the trains were designed you would first get twisted one way and then you were slammed against one side. And before you could brace yourself, you were slammed against the other side. This is what unnerved some and delighted others. There were always three trains running on the Bobs so that the crowds would be kept moving without too long a wait. Whether or not you rode in the front, last or middle seat you always held on for dear life. Did you ever wonder what an astronaut experienced during weightlessness? Well, if you had ever ridden the Bobs, you had the chance to get a slight feeling of what it was like. Let me give you an example, a 150 pound man would weigh 400 pounds going down hill on the Bobs and because of gravity that same 150 pound man would weigh only 15 pounds on top. Once again the daddy of them all, THE BOBS.

WHICH WAS ROUGHER—CYCLONE OR BOBS

Some say the Cyclone Coaster at Coney Island in New York was faster and rougher than the Bobs, but then again some say the Bobs took first place. The Cyclone is still up and running in New York, so if you have been on the Bobs go to Coney Island and take a ride on the Cyclone and judge for yourself. The big difference from what I can see is the price. Remember I mentioned that you could ride the Bobs for 35¢ to 50¢ for the first ride and 25¢ to 35¢ for the second and additional rides, the Cyclone will cost about $1.00 per ride.

Another of my favorites, is the next ride you come to on riverwalk, the Flying Scooter. This was a portable type ride, very similar to the Stratostat, only smaller. You can control this type of plane, by using the handle of the big rudder that was up in front. This handle could be used to move you high or low or wherever the rider wanted to fly. Once the Flying Scooter ride came into Riverview it never changed its location. Before the Flying Scooter, the racing coaster called the Jack Rabbit was located on this spot, but that was before 1935.

Loading up the Flying Scooters. You could fly these planes yourself. (C. Wlodarczyk)

49

Continuing around the corner, (that is prior to 1948) you would see a ride called the Moon Rocket. The ride consisted of a circle of cars all connected together, sitting on a table tilted 30 degrees. Once the Moon Rocket started, the cars would circle the tracks building up speed and at the same time the cars would be going up and down. The ride went so fast that you felt like you were climbing to the moon. Maybe that's where the name came from, the Moon Rocket. A Moon Rocket ride can be found at Dandelion Park in Muskego, Wisconsin, a suburb of Milwaukee. A nice ride, but only for those who like stomach-churning rides.

Sometime after 1948 when the Moon Rocket was removed, the Hot Rods occupied this location. Maybe I can help refresh your memory of the Hot Rods. The little cars were always popular, especially with the kids who looked forward to driving their own car. The Hot Rods were similar to the Go-Kart rides of today. They were lots of fun for people of all ages! Actually the land that the Flying Scooter, the Hot Rods and the Moon Rocket were all on was the entire site of Jack Rabbit Roller Coaster. Many old-time Riverview buffs remember the Jack Rabbit and are always asking about the coaster. The reason for taking the Jack Rabbit down was because a fire in the 1930's damaged part of the ride's structure.

The old Moon Rocket ride ran its last season in 1948 and was replaced by the Hot Rods. (W. Smith)

From this position in the park we find that we are right behind the back end of the Riverview Roller Rink. On hot summer nights, we could enjoy an extra treat. What was it? The windows and doors of the rink would be opened for ventilation and we could look in and see the skaters and possibly hear the *Skater's Waltz* played by the organist, Russ Young. The roller rink remained standing after the park closed, but was eventually destroyed by fire a couple of years later.

After taking a relaxing break, are you ready to continue our walk in the "world's largest amusement park"? Right about here we come upon a Penny Arcade. Few people know or remember that the building that housed the games was, in fact, the old entrance to Jack Rabbit racing coaster.

We make a left turn and here we start walking down the walkway called the Bowery. In later years this was where many portable type rides could be found. The portable rides in the Bowery area could be moved to other locations in the park.

If we would go back several years in our memories, the first ride we would come to on the Bowery would be the Ginger Snap, Virginia Reel or finally the Crazy Ribbon. The Crazy Ribbon had barrel shaped cars, similar to those of the Boomerang cars. When the ride began you rode up an inclined track to the top, once there on top,

This aerial view shows why the last name of this ride was the most appropriate one it had at Riverview, it was called the Crazy Ribbon.
(W. Smith)

The Flying Saucer at the start of the Bowery offers an angle of the Pair-O-Chutes.
(C. Wlodarczyk)

51

you rolled and twisted back and forth from one side to the other. The floor was pitched so that each time you would twist back and forth, the movement of the cars was actually taking you back to where you originally got on the car, that is at safe level ground. The Crazy Ribbon was very popular. However, it was still taken down in the late 1940's. The name Crazy Ribbon was really most fitting because if you were riding the Pair-O-Chutes and looked down, it looked like someone took a ribbon and twisted it all over a large table with loops at each end.

Remember the Calypso, not the dance but the ride. Here it is, spinning merrily in a blur of lights at night. (C. Wlodarczyk)

Remember the Cat game? Cat-Mop heads sat there, waiting for someone to knock them down. Many tried to win but only a few did.
(C. Wlodarczyk)

52

The Crazy Ribbon was replaced by a portable type ride called the Flying Saucer. The Flying Saucer lasted at the park until the early 1960's. Let me describe it to you in case you don't remember it. The Flying Saucer had two big arms with circular platforms at each end. People sat in the circular end of the arms and when the ride began the arms spun around giving you a whiplike sensation as the ride continued.

After the Flying Saucer was removed, the new ride that replaced it was Mountain Road. Have you ever been on a ride like the Super Himalaya found at carnivals or fairs? If you have, then you would know what the Mountain Road was like. The Mountain Road didn't last very long, however, and was soon replaced by the Twist. The Twist was a short lived ride, too. It was only there two seasons when the park closed in 1967. It was a portable, carnival type ride also.

The Bowery area contained many rides and attractions over the years till the closing in 1967. Let's review some of them. Where the Twist was located, the Octopus once stood, but maybe some remember the Derby coaster, this is the area that was covered by the Derby Coaster. During the years the Looper, the Flying Cars, Fly-O-Planes, the Up and Over Cages (still found today in various parks and carnivals) Calypso and also Kiddyland #2. (See next page.) Kiddyland #2 had another great assortment of rides for kids, similar to Kiddyland #1 on the main midway.

Some of the other attractions which were found on the Bowery were games of chance such as the Fish Pond, the Pop Guns, the Dart Throw, Hammer the Nail and the list goes on and on. The Bowery also was where you could find the Jitterbug Fun House during the 1940's. Out in front you could find a fat lady mannequin. The mannequin swayed and rocked and shook while a recording blared laughter which went along with her movements. Come on in and see what's inside, that is if you have the nerve.

The African Dip was also on the Bowery through the 1950's. Remember how hard you would work to hit those targets so that you could dunk the man that heckled you. The black men in the cages really knew how to get to you. Sometimes they would get you so mad that you'd throw the balls at the cages rather than the targets. If you were heavy, they'd call you meatball. If you were thin, they might have called you toothpick. If you were with a girl, they might have said "Hey fella, that ain't the same girl you were with yesterday." They were successful, since you never left after throwing only a couple of balls. You almost always kept it up until you got them wet. Their job kept them wet, but financially secure since they made a couple of hundred dollars a week. Back then that was big money. It was all for fun and you had the chance to get your anxieties out for 10 or 25 cents.

Walking on down the Bowery and at the end of the walk on one corner, the Boomerang was housed. After waiting in line, which by the way was worth it, you climbed into round tub-shaped cars. The seats were so narrow you would wonder how on earth you were going to be able to sit on it while the ride was moving. Before you could think about it very long, you were hooked onto a spinning turntable. Spinning around and around you forgot how narrow the seat in the car was because all you were concerned with at this point was just holding on TIGHT! All of a sudden you left the turntable and you were flung through a U-shaped tunnel, still spinning and twisting. Coming out of the tunnel, you were kind of glad the ride was over. Want to ride again?

If you could stand up after the ride, you would cross the Bowery to the Greyhound roller coaster. Remember riding in open-topped cars (of course, the last seat again) on Riverview's baby coaster. It was a baby coaster compared to the other coasters in the park, especially the Bobs, but it was one of the longest coasters with tracks reaching

Gliding over the Boomerang in the Space Ride car, we see the cars being loaded. (C. Wlodarczyk)

all the way to Belmont Avenue. It was a smooth ride that could be enjoyed because of the mild dips and the two tunnels on the long track surface. Also for only 5¢ to 20¢ how could you pass it up. A few seasons before the park's closing, the Greyhound had a name change. The Jetstream was created by rebuilding tracks and replacing the Greyhound trains with new ones and also making the ride shorter by taking some of the tracks out. It still was a mild roller coaster ride, however. The Jetstream was one of Riverview's losers in the money area. Like the Space Ride and the Twist it never really paid for its remodeling.

Continuing on in our memory tour of Riverview, we leave the Greyhound or Jetstream ride. Making a bend in the walk, get some money out because there are some more games to play. Stop and play for awhile!

All finished? Ready to continue on? If this was prior to 1950, we would come up to the Tumble Bug. The Tumble Bug had cars similar in shape to the Boomerang cars. The cars though were hooked together in a circle and glided up and down mild dips rather slowly. A nice ride but it too was replaced.

The old Greyhound entrance shows people waiting to board the mild roller coaster. Also the boomerang cars are being hooked onto the turntable for their spin around. (C. Wlodarczyk)

As we see the Greyhound train climbing, notice the backend view of the Calypso. The Greyhound was the longest roller coaster in track footage in the park. You can get some idea from this shot — just look at the wooden structure. (C. Wlodarczyk)

The Greyhound train made it to the top of its first hill, it was mostly downhill from then on. You can see the Calypso ride and also the ill-fated Mountain Road under the striped roof. (J. Kolberg)

The Greyhound is gone and the completely new JetStream is in its spot. The JetStream was a shorter ride and everything was new, only it did not make the money that had been expected. (L. Daunis)

IT WAS FUN EVEN IF WE DID GET WET!

Replaced it was by another popular favorite, the Water Bug. Ready to cool off again? You are going to get wet! The Water Bug was composed of little gasoline operated boats with large inner tube bumpers. Like the Bump-Em, the fun part of the Water Bug was to bump people in the other cars or boats, the difference though was that you were bound to get wet by the splashing. Don't worry about drowning in the deep water though, it was only a couple of feet deep. Sorry, the reasonably priced (15 to 25¢) Water Bug ride is over; time to move on! Get your hankies out and dry your face.

The sputtering, puttering Water Bugs glide and bump across the pool. Skee Ball and Rifle range in the background were enjoyed by thousands each season. (C. Wlodarczyk)

Before going on another ride let's stop at Skee Ball since it's just across the walkway. Wouldn't it be fun to win a giant stuffed toy? Skee Ball is similar to a bowling game. At Riverview for 5¢ or 10¢ you would get 9 balls to roll up an alley aiming for bins at the end. Each bin had varying point values, usually from 10 to 50 points. Naturally the higher the score the better chance you had to win bigger prizes. Actually you received tickets according to your score which you could accumulate during the entire season which really was a good idea. This way, by the end of the season you probably had enough tickets to get something really nice. You may have played Skee Ball at Riverview, but if not, don't feel cheated. Try playing it at other amusement parks, lots of them have Skee Ball.

PAIR-O-CHUTES IS BIGGEST ON CHUTES WALK

Our day of fun and adventure continues now, walking down Chutes walk we see how this part of our journey got its name. Before our eyes we see a sight all Chicagoans recognized as synonymous with Riverview, the Pair-O-Chutes. Indeed an overwhelming sight, frightening possibly to some, enjoyable to millions. More about the Pair-O-Chutes when we reach that ever so high ride. We have more to see and ride before getting there. We are now in an area that had many portable type rides such as: the Jet Rockets, the Rollo Plane, the Rock-O-Plane, the Octopus and finally the Rotor.

↖This photo was taken in 1948 from the Pair-O-Chutes. It shows Chutes walk before the Rotor; the Tumble Bug had already been replaced by the Water Bug. You can see the Roll-O-Plane and Octopus though, in the area where the Rotor would occupy a few years later. (J. Kolberg)

The Jet Rockets whirl around and flood lights shine on the Rotor in this night scene. (J. Kolberg) ⟶

All these rides were on the west side of Chutes walk because on the east side the park provided benches so that we could rest our weary feet. Behind the benches you could relax just watching the Duck Pond and enjoy the lovely gardens that were located there. If you watched the pond a while, you might catch a glimpse of the paddle wheel Showboat ride which floated there, or a glimpse of the one legged duck that was at the park for years. Reports were the duck lost its leg when it was run over by the train.

The Showboats share space with permanent resident ducks in the pond, in this view taken from atop of the Pair-O-Chutes. You get a good look at the Flash tracks and the Fireball trackage.
(C. Wlodarczyk)

After resting you are ready to ride again? You start by going over to the Jet Rockets. This ride had rocket-shaped ships that revolved in a circle and while circling in the air the ships were hydraulically raised or lowered.

On a busy day in 1956, the Jet Rockets, the Rotor and the Pair-O-Chutes are all operating.
(C. Wlodarczyk)

59

After leaving the Jet Rocket, let's take a ride on the Rock-O-Plane, that is if our stomachs can take it. At first glance, you notice that the Rock-O-Plane resembled a ferris wheel, after riding it you would soon find out that is where the comparison ended. The riders on the Rock-O-Plane were enclosed in cage type cars and as the ride began the riders could spin the cars individually by stepping on the lever located on the floor of each car. So the Rock-O-Plane went around in a ferris wheel fashion but you could really spin your heads off.

When you got off the Rock-O-Plane you had to be dizzy, so since you were already dizzy you might as well take on another stomach twister. If you have ever been on one at a carnival, you know what I'm talking about! The Octopus was ready for you. Its many arms held two compartments of two cars each. As the Octopus began, you find yourself going up and down and spinning and twisting. Really it was quite like the Tilt-A-Whirl in the spinning and twisting. The ride is over, are you ready for more spinning? Join me right next door!

You are probably hearing a loud speaker about now, with people screaming and laughing. Also there is a man standing outside a well-lighted building, telling people to come on in and have the thrill of your life. If you got over some of your dizziness by this time, you would go in. It seemed so inviting, so why not? The man said you watch or ride for 20¢ to 30¢. So as long as we have the choice, we'll watch first then ride. Have you guessed which ride I'm talking about yet? If not, I won't keep you in suspense any longer, it is the Rotor.

One of the newspaper ads used to draw crowds to Riverview before 1967.

FUN FOR ALL!

2¢ DAYS! MON., WED., FRI., (except holidays)

NO INCREASE IN PRICES

5¢ NITES! TUES., THURS.,

America's Famous AMUSEMENT PARK
RIVERVIEW
WESTERN-BELMONT

60

The **Pair-O-Chutes Tower looms high over all** other rides in the park.
(C. Wlodarczyk)

From our vantage point we could see people entering a large barrel through a door which would soon be shut. Once inside, the people were told to stand against the wall when the ride started the barrel would begin to spin faster and faster, as the speed increased the floor suddenly dropped to a few feet below, but strangely the people didn't. This is when you could hear screams. The people were plastered against the walls due to centrifugal force.

That's where the people stayed until the ride started to slow down When the ride slowed down the floor would rise slowly to meet their feet. Those watching could see an extra sight, an unexpected one, the ladies with skirts on always had problems about now, as the ride slowed down their bodies had a tendancy to slide down a little. The problem came in because the skirts didn't slide they stayed plastered to the wall. Here's where the unexpected extra came in you got to see a little more leg than you had expected. I'm sure many ladies had wished they wore slacks in those days.

Now it is my turn to ride the Rotor. I did and the feeling pinned against the spinning walls was a weird sensation, you really had a feeling of sliding down at times. When the ride on the Rotor was over I decided that my first ride was going to be my last on this one. Never again, not on a Rotor—once getting sick for me was enough.

KEEP PLENTY OF CHANGE TO PLAY GAMES

Let's let our stomachs calm down a bit and play some games. Try the Coke Bottle toss first. Two coke bottles were placed about 4 feet from you and you were given two chances to knock the bottles down with a ball about the size of a league ball. It sure looked easy, but you soon found out it only looked easy. Oh well, maybe we'll win at another game. There was always the Basketball toss where you had two out of three chances to win, maybe you'd prefer the Cat toss game, remember they looked like mopheads lined up on shelves and all you had to do was knock them down with a ball. The next game guaranteed you a prize, it was the string pulling game. There were all sorts of nice prizes on the end of strings; stuffed animals, plaster dolls, etc. All you had to do was select a string out of about a hundred that were held by the concessionaire. Of course not all of the strings held real good prizes but even a small trinket was better than nothing. It was all for fun anyway.

Moving on, we have finally reached the monster of all the rides, the Pair-O-Chutes, looming 212 feet above the ground. Originally the Pair-O-Chutes was an observation tower called the Eye-Ful tower. Right up the center of the tower ran an elevator which carried people to the top for a view of Chicago. The city condemned the elevator saying it was unsafe to transport people, so for many years, in fact until 1937, the tower was all that was really there. But then in 1937 after determining that the structure itself was quite safe and strong, the park made the former Eye-Ful tower into the Pair-O-Chutes as we remember it. It was then that the spans were added to accommodate the chutes. It soon became one of the park's favorite rides.

Are you aware that the Pair-O-Chutes set a record in amusement park history? The Pair-O-Chutes at Riverview was a first of a kind. It was the first free-fall parachute ride to be constructed. There are now two operating Pair-O-Chute type rides around and one that does not operate any longer. The one that does not operate any longer came from the New York World's Fair and later operated at Steeplechase Park in Coney Island. That one was a free-fall type. The other two Pair-O-Chute type rides look similar to the Pair-O-Chutes of Riverview fame, but they are not free-fall type. One opened last year at Six Flags Over Georgia and is called the Gasp and the other is located at Knottsberry Farm in Buena Park, California, and it is called the

Parachute Sky Jump. Getting back to Riverview, the Pair-O-Chutes operated from 1937-1967, giving millions of people a thrill beyond their wildest expectations. Just standing at the base of the tower almost unnerved us, we would certainly need to build up courage to take the chance on riding, knowing that once you started up you couldn't get off till the ride was over. The Pair-O-Chutes was a trouble-free ride with very few operating problems. The only problems really, were the operators themselves. They enjoyed people's discomfort, especially if they saw that you were shaky when you were boarding the ride. They would let you climb perhaps three quarters of the way up and then they would cut the power ... scary to say the least! If you had the nerve to look down, the operator would be giving you the sign like they didn't know what happened or what was wrong. If you wanted to impress your date with bravery, you could have always slipped the operator some money and he would do the same thing to you too. Then when the chute stopped, you would be brave and unafraid and your date would fall into your arms frightened to death and of course impressed with your bravery. After a few seconds, which would seem like an hour, the ride would begin again, the power being turned back on. You would once again begin your slow climb to the 196 foot level or the top. Reaching the top after what seemed like an eternity, you would suddenly receive a JOLT and for a second you felt like the seat fell from beneath you. A seat, by the way, that really didn't look like it would hold you anyway. It was only small webbed canvas straps behind and underneath you and a canvas strap bar across your lap. While sailing down in a free fall, you felt sure your finger prints would be left on that rubber bar on each side because you were holding on so tightly. Then suddenly another JOLT a few seconds after the first, only this time you were on the bottom. You hit the bottom so hard that when you hit the coil springs you would bounce up so high that it almost felt like you were going back up to the top again. With wobbly knees you would get off the Pair-O-Chutes and walk away saying to yourself "Never again"—but that really wasn't true. You knew the next time at the park you'd ride again. After all, half the fun was getting scared wasn't it?????

From the base of the Chutes Tower looking straight up 212 feet, we can see the lace work of steel. The Pair-O-Chutes were a long-time landmark of Chicago's Northside.
(C. Wlodarczyk)

The steel structure of the Pair-O-Chutes stood 212 feet high. (C. Wlodarczyk)

On the day this picture was shot the winds were so strong the Pair-O-Chutes weren't operating, but you can still see the crowds didn't stay away. (C. Wlodarczyk)

I used the Pair-O-Chutes to get many of the aerial photographs you see in the book, because the view was undeniably spectacular. I asked the operator to take me up to the top and kill the power for a few minutes. In this way I could concentrate on getting photographs rather than the jolt on top.

Leaving the Pair-O-Chutes, many wanted to find a bench and sit for awhile and let some color come back to their faces. Others who were strong and had also ridden the Pair-O-Chutes before were ready to take on more fun and thrills right away.

In these four pictures we'll be riding the Pair-O-Chutes, so hang onto your hats. Notice the photo gallery where you might have had your picture taken on the moon or on the train or perhaps at the bar. (C. Wlodarczyk)

Up we go, halfway
up we can look around
and see many of
Riverview's attrac-
tions. (C. Wlodarczyk)

Up near the top of
the Pair-O-Chutes
we can see for miles.
Hang on we'll be
dropping down soon.
(C. Wlodarczyk)

Up on top we have a
moment to look
around and see the
main gate on Western
Avenue, and we get a
nice view of the
Showboat pond.
(J. Kolberg)

66

Walking down Castle walk we move to the Bughouse; that is, if you were around Riverview before the 1930's. The Bughouse was a fun house that you could have spent the entire day in, and it would have only cost you 15¢. The Bughouse had giant slides in it. On the slides you would ride down to the bottom over bumpy hills on a carpet provided by the operator on top. You might also have enjoyed the Sugar Bowl which you sat on and spun around on. However, if you stayed on too long you would receive an electric shock to get you off and it did move you off. The Bughouse burned down in the 1930's either '30 or '31. Too bad, but it was replaced by an all-time favorite of Riverview buffs, Aladdin's Castle. Want to join me while we go on through?

THE CASTLE

After paying for a ticket which was always reasonable only 15¢ or 20¢, you started your tour through a maze of screen doors. It took you a while to get through because all the doors looked the same and you always pushed the wrong door and there was a dead end. The castle had a mirror room, inside this room you could look fat, skinny, tall or short, depending on which mirror you wanted to look in. It also had a room with slanted floors. I can walk through without holding onto the railings you would say, but soon found out that was easier said than done. Everyone usually held on at least part way through the room.

There were countless dark corridors in the castle that sure added to the fun you were having. Halfway through we come across the floor that had round discs that twirled when you stepped on them. This too looked easy to cross, but it wasn't. Remember the rolling barrel in the castle, you thought you could run right through, but if you had no practice in passing through then you probably ended up on the seat of your pants. I remember when I was young, trying to figure out how some got through and others would fall like I did. After analyzing the situation for several seasons and many times falling in the barrel, I finally thought I had it figured down pat. Down pat was descriptive too because that's how I ended up many times even after having figured it out. You had to determine which way the barrel was rolling and then walk at the same angle it was turning. If you were swift enough you probably made it through, if not, then you ended up falling and laughing your head off. The barrel would stop all of a sudden and you would get out. The operator had to stop the barrel to prevent any serious accidents. However, if you wanted to prevent any falling, laughing and just plain fun you could have just taken the walk through the door next to the barrel and then you would have come out right next to the barrel.

AIR LIFTED LADIES SKIRTS

Do you remember the stairway outside the building? Remember climbing right past Aladdin's beard! If you were a lady with a skirt on, I'm sure you do. There were two or three air hoses embedded in the stairs. The stairs led to some more fun in the Castle and since there was no other way to get there, you had to climb the stairs. Generally the people were unsuspecting as they climbed them, anxious to get to some more fun. It was here that the air hoses would do the job that they were intended to do. When a lady started climbing the stairs all of a sudden a blast of air, up went the skirts and roars of laughter from the crowds of people that had gathered out in front could be heard. Embarrassed the lady would turn bright red and finish climbing the stairs, but you can sure bet she was holding tightly onto her skirt.

At the top of the stairs, there was a porch where you turned to go back into the castle; climbing the few more stairs the ladies felt they were safe now so they would let their guard down and let go of their skirts. Unknown to most people here is where a big blast of air would get those poor unsuspecting women. They would be on those stairs into the castle and the big blast of air would startle them and skirts would bellow out and up once again to the screams of the hundreds watching. All this fun was done by a merciless fellow sitting in the little booth or room located above the pay windows. He would sit there and catch those poor women to the roar and applause of the onlookers. Didn't he have a tough job???

Getting back inside the castle, we have more dark, scary passageways to tour. Down we go, down big padded rollers actually resembling a large slide only soft and bumpy. Wasn't that fun? It was to me but if you didn't like the looks of that, then you could always walk down the stairs alongside the bumper rollers. The rooms and corridors in Aladdin's Castle were so much fun, I can still imagine being there. Now remember arriving at the Magic Carpet, sad to say this is the end of Aladdin's Castle but what an end! If you decided to ride the Magic Carpet out you would sit on a slick metal seat that collapsed when the operator pulled the lever. Then down you go on

This picture of Aladdin's Castle was taken the same year the Space Ride was installed, if you can see the sign in the parking lot on Belmont it announced the new Space Ride. Notice Chicago's skyline didn't have many super tall buildings. (C. Wlodarczyk)

the moving carpet over rollers bouncing and laughing to the end of the carpet and then down a small slide. After exiting, are you ready to go through Aladdin's Castle again? I am . . .

In later years the Magic Carpet was removed which was a real shame because it certainly was a bundle of fun. The only reason I can figure that it was removed (but I really can't say for sure) was that clothing may have been ripped too often.

In this photo you can see where the man who operated the air hoses on the stairs sat, in the building in the foreground. The door at the top of the stairs to the left of the beard was where all the action took place.
(C. Wlodarczyk)

This shot gives an idea of just how big Aladdin's Castle really was. It had to be, to hold all the things that I mentioned. (J. Kolberg)

Once out of the castle we continue our day of fun at Riverview, but first our eyes have to adjust to the lights. Pausing and squinting, we see our next ride as we walk toward Western Avenue. We can see the Super Eli. Super it was indeed, it was an extra high Ferris Wheel, in fact twice the height of regular Ferris Wheels. It was located at this spot until 1963, when it was moved to the Bowery area. It was moved to make room for the East platform of the Space Ride.

After getting off the Super Eli we note that Western Avenue is parallel to us and if we are ready to play some games we could pause for a while and see if we can win a stuffed Majorette or a Kewpie Doll. If not, we could continue walking on to Ophelia's Paradise, or maybe you remember it being called Spooktown. I know you remember the last name this ride had: "Ghost Train." We would climb aboard the little cars with a friend or two and then go through the swinging doors into darkness again. Only this time in the darkness you would see monster figures leaping out at you, hear eerie noises and feel creepy things touching you. Of course, what you felt were only ropes hanging down, but in the dark you weren't sure, after all who was about to reach up and touch it to make sure. Who cared by that time anyway! A popular sound in the Ghost Train was screaming, you sure could hear all the girls in the other cars. They were scared to death but were brave and not afraid ... Weren't We! Before you knew it we could see a crack of light and suddenly doors swung open and you were outside again.

Bravely we walk on to a ride that maybe our bravery could take, but possibly not our stomachs. A few years back the Dive Bomber was situated right here and up to the end of 1967 the Roll-O-Plane churned our stomachs in this location. If we weren't quite up to riding just yet, we could stand and watch others or we could play a few

Here is Ghost Train or Spook Town. In the background you can see the main gate again.
(J. Kolberg)

Looks like a Halloween picture but it **really** is just the final paint job on the Ghost Train.
(L. Daunis)

71

more games while our courage got stronger. Oh well, no sense putting it off; let's get in line for the Dive Bomber. Do you remember this ride? If you were ever on it I'm quite sure you didn't forget it, but just in case let me refresh your memory. The Dive Bomber could seat 8 to 12 people during one ride in both of its two capsule-shaped cars. That meant two or three people sat in front and back of each car. After you had been buckled in, the cars would begin swinging in opposite directions. The swinging would get you higher and higher until you were upside down, even being locked up there till you begged the operator to let you down. The Roll-O-Plane which came to this spot in later years was actually quite similar to the Dive Bomber. It didn't swing. However, it did get you right to the top, that is upside down. At the same time you were upside down you were being rolled from side to side, as if you really needed that. If you could walk when you got off either of these rides, you might have wanted to sit a spell which seemed like a good idea at the time.

After your stomach got back in place you could play some games, maybe one like Ring-the-Bell or others. In any case the ride you just got off was one that the operators liked, they were always cleaning up on these rides, but not what you think they cleaned up. When you were on top, upside down, more than likely the change you had in your pocket fell out and scattered on the ground under the planes, so the operators would add to their financial status by sweeping the ground under the Dive Bomber or the Roll-O-Plane. Both of these rides were popular among the operators and you can see why.

The Roll-O-Plane spins and dips to the delights of the people watching, but I wonder if we can say the same for the people riding?
(C. Wlodarczyk)

Are you still dizzy? If you are, wait a few more minutes because you needed a good eye to play the Goldfish and Bird game. Remember all the little bowls lined up on shelves. Some of them had goldfish in them and a few had birds painted on them. You always aimed for the bird bowls with the ping-pong balls you were given but more than likely you landed your ball in the goldfish bowl. That meant you took home a goldfish. If your ball landed in the bird bowl you could have taken home a parakeet. How many did you win?

Are you hungry now? There are some concession stands right here and we could always grab a snack. While snacking you'd have to decide if you were going home or if your legs could walk some more, because sad to say our tour of Riverview "the World's Largest Amusement Park" has ended. Of course, you could always tour the midway again!!!

72

1904-1967

By

Chuck Wlodarczyk

Interesting Facts You Would Like to Know:

1. A Brief History of Riverview
2. Technical Information
3. List of Rides with Name Changes
4. Operating Schedule
5. Special Group Outings
6. Insurance and Accident Rates
7. Miscellaneous Information
8. Comments on Other Amusement Parks

Brief History of Riverview

Did you know that Riverview Amusement Park was originally the location of a garbage dump? Maybe your memory brings the name German Sharpshooter Park to mind. If so, you are right. Actually on July 2, 1904, the gates to Riverview, "the world's largest amusement park," were opened. At that time horse drawn cars pulled people to the old German Sharpshooter Park, a hunting preserve, with targets set up on an island in the river and with plenty of deer lurking in the woods.

Many of us rode these old but reliable, non-pollutent street cars to Riverview. Car lines serving the park were: Western, Belmont, Clybourn and Roscoe. (E. Frank, Jr.)

Riverview was always a family project or enterprise owned by the Schmidt family: Wilhelm Schmidt, George Schmidt and William Schmidt, Jr. The park, as we remember it, got its real beginning after Wilhelm or William, Sr., started hearing complaints from the members' wives. The wives complained that there was nothing for them to do, while their husbands talked about how good their shooting was and while they were consuming their brew.

Mr. Schmidt decided that he would put a Merry-Go-Round in the park to help quiet their complaints and give the wives and children something to do. In 1906 he

These tickets and prices bring back memories, don't they? If you read from left to right and top to bottom you'd know which way the rides were laid out. (C. Wlodarczyk)

comissioned a group of Swiss-Italian wood carvers, employed by the Philadelphia Toboggan company, to fashion a carousel. Once the Carousel was set up its location was never changed. Not one of the 70 prancing horses were ever replaced, just repainted. In all the years of Riverview, millions of children of all ages would hurry to ride, going nowhere, and squabble over which beautiful horse they were to mount. Were you one?

It was around this time, that George Schmidt returned from Europe, enthused by what he had seen and enjoyed while overseas. He came back full of ideas on amusement parks. It was at this time that Riverview started to grow and spread out

76

with rides and attractions of all types to become the world's largest amusement park. In 1967, if George Schmidt had lived to see his dream, he would have enjoyed, as we did, the more than 33 rides and numerous other attractions.

Riverview did have its ups and downs in more ways than just rides. During the depression years, Riverview suffered too. Those were lean years for the park as well as for everyone else. But during the war years, Riverview thrived, it was financially successful then.

AUCTION

RIVERVIEW PARK
WORLDS LARGEST AMUSEMENT PARK

FRIDAY, DECEMBER 1st - 11 a. m.
3300 North Western Avenue

$3,000,000
27 AMUSEMENT PARK RIDES

SPACE RIDES AND EQUIPMENT - IMPORTED HAND CARVED European Craftsmanship HORSES MOUNTED ON MERRY GO ROUND (Collectors Showpiece)

TILT-A-WHIRL	STREAMLINER TRAINS
FLASH HIGH RIDE	CATERPILLAR
FIREBALL	SAFARI
OLD MILL STREAM (TUNNEL OF LOVE)	CHUTE-RIDE
KIDDYLAND	WHIP
CRAZY DAZY	COMETRIDE WITH CARS
STRATOSTAT	MERRY-GO-ROUND
THE BOBS (WORLD FAMOUS)	FLYING TURNS
HOT RODS (35 CARS)	TWIST
WATERBUG	JET STREAM WITH CARS
PAIR O CHUTES	ALADDINS CASTLE
SPACE RIDE	GHOST TRAIN
ROLLO PLANE	ARCADES

(Maintenance Equipment, Tools, Machine Shop, Hardware, etc., etc., to be sold at a later date to be announced).

INSPECTION: WED. & THUR. - NOV. 29th & 30th
10:00 a. m. to 4:00 p. m.

When the gates were finally locked and closed in the fall of 1967, the park was said to have grossed more than 2½ million dollars. That doesn't seem all that much you say? Remember however, that inflation hadn't hit like we know it today and also that the park only operated for four months or 118 days. It was reported that on a good day, Riverview could bring in as much as $65,000.00 in the 1950's or 1960's. I'll let you escalate these figures into today's cost structure. Probably the figures today would be around 8 to 10 million dollars gross for the same period of time.

Riverview was truly a wonderful melting pot for people of all races and nationalities, old and young. It was the happy meeting ground for the young in age and also the young in heart. We all miss it, Don't we?

DEMOLITION SCENES

Inside Main Gate taken after park was closed. (J. Kolberg from collection of K. Reiger)

The turnstyles had seen much wear over the years but never looked sadder than during the demolition. (J. Kolberg from collection of K. Reiger)

The Flying Turns in the winter of 1967. Or what was left of the Flying Turns that is. (J. Kolberg from collection of K. Reiger)

78

Looking down this Main Midway several months earlier you would have seen thousands enjoying themselves for the last time. Demolition of Riverview couldn't have been a happy job. (J. Kolberg from collection of K. Reiger)

Almost looks as if Aladdin knows what was in store for him seeing the crumpled Pair-O-Chutes Tower on the ground. (J. Kolberg from collection of K. Reiger)

The wild first hill of the Bobs is finally tamed by the wrecking crew. (J. Kolberg from collection of K. Reiger)

It was truly a sad day when this long-time landmark of the Northwest side and Riverview came tumbling down. (J. Kolberg from collection of K. Reiger)

The 200 foot Pair-O-Chutes Tower is sent crashing down. (J. Kolberg from collection of K. Reiger)

"B YY's" come on Bargain Days to Riverview, don't we wish we still could? (J. Kolberg from collection of K. Reiger)

Safety-Conscious Riverview Tested All Rides Frequently

The following information shows the testing procedures used prior to opening the park each season (this one happened to be for 1952). All the rides were thoroughly tested so that accidents would be prevented. Each day the rides were also tested by having dry runs. Riverview was very anti-accident conscious, which really showed up through their accident record.

TECHNICAL AND STRUCTURAL SPECIFICATIONS

TILT-A-WHIRL — 100% Overload.
9 Cars, Seating 27 people.
6 Sand Bags to a Car — Total Sand Bag test 5400 lb.

SILVER FLASH — 100% Overload.
Approximately 2583 ft. coaster ride.
Time of ride approximately 1 minute 45 seconds.
2 trains to the ride, 4 Coaches to a train,
Seating 24 people. Sand Bag Test Load 7200 lb.

DOUBLE FERRIS WHEEL — 33½% Overload.
2 Separate Ferris Wheels, 12 seats to a Ferris Wheel. Seating 48 people to the ride.
Sand test load 6000 lb. to a wheel, 5 sand bags to a car.

SPOOKTOWN
1 Horse power motor driven ride.
10 cars to the ride, 2 seats to a car.
Seating 20 people to the ride.

DODGEM
¼ Horse Power Motor cars — individually operated.
1 person to a car, 58 cars to the ride.
Approximately seating 44 people when rides operates.

BLUE STREAK — 100% Overload.
Approximately 2800 ft. coaster ride.
Time of ride approximately 2 minutes 5 seconds.
2 trains to the ride, 3 coaches to a train.
Seating 24 people, Sand Bag test load 7200 lb.

MINIATURE RAILROAD
2 Trains to the ride, 7 Coaches to a train.
Approximately 2500 ft. of track.
6 seats to a coach — seating 12 persons.
Seating 84 persons to a train.

CATERPILLAR
23 Seats to the ride, Seating 48 people.
4 bags to a seat, Total Sand Bag Test 9600 lb.

CHUTES — 66⅔% Overload.
1 Boat seating 10 people.
Approximately normal load 1500 lb.
Car speed 195 feet per minute.
Sand Test Load 2500 lb.
1 Elevator machine serving 2 elevator cradle cars (north & south). North & south cradle car safety tested with 1500 lb. of sand each car.
Car safety shoes changed from Keastner Hecht type to Reliance type by Reliance Elevator Co.

TUNNEL OF LOVE
Water Boat Ride.
1 Boat seating 10 people, 10 Boats to the Ride.

WHIP — 33⅓% Overload.
15 Cars to the ride, 2 persons to a car.
Seating 30 people.
Sand test load 6000 lb., 4 Sand Bags to a car.

KIDDYLAND
4 miniature rides, 1 Kiddy Whip — 8 cars.
1 Kiddy Merry-Go-Round — 24 horses.
1 Kiddy Boat Ride — 6 boats.
1 Kiddy Tumble Bug — 3 tubs.

CUDDLE UP
11 tubs to the ride, Seating 44 people.
Test Load 5600 lb., 6 Sand Bags to a tub.

COMET — 100% Overload.
Approximately 3000 ft. Coaster ride.
Time of ride approximately 2 minutes, 12 seconds.
3 Trains to the ride.
4 Coaches to a Train, each seating 24 people.
Sand test load 7200 lb.

HADES
Wooden Structure, Walk Around Fun Devices
7 fire exits.

STRATOSTAT — 33⅓% Overload.
3 Ships to the ride, Seating 36 people.
Normal load approximately 5400 lb.
Sand Test Load 7200 lb.

MERRY-GO-ROUND
70 Horses seating 70, 4 Lover's Chariots seating 30. Total seating 100 people.

FLYING TURNS — 100% Overload.
5 cars to a train.
Approximately 1300 ft. barrel coaster ride.
Time of ride approximately 1 minute, 55 seconds.
Some loss time in barrel roll.
Seating 10 people.
Normal live load approximately 1500 lb.
Sand Test Load 3000 lb.

BOBS — 100% Overload.
Approximately 3300 ft. coaster ride.
Time of ride approximately 2 minutes, 7 seconds.
3 trains to a ride, 11 coaches to a train.
Seating 22 people.
Sand test load 6600 lb.

BUBBLE BOUNCE — Live load.
8 Cars to the ride, 4 people to a car.
Seating 32 people total.
Test live load approximately 5000 lb.

FLYING SCOOTER — 100% Overload.
10 Ships to the ride, seating 20 people.
Normal live load approximately 3000 lb.
Sand test load 6000 lb., 6 sand bags to ship.

KIDDIE AUTO RIDE
54 Cars, seating 54 Children.
Repairs — Drive Cable Renewed.

FLYING SAUCER — 25% Overload.
2 Revolving platforms 16 people to a platform.
32 people to the ride.
Normal live load approximately 4800 lb.
Tested with 6000 lb. of sand.

MOTORSYNDROME
Motorcycle Show, Observation platform.
Wooden Structure.

FLY-O-PLANE — Live load.
8 Ships, 2 people to a ship.
Seating 16 people to the ride.

GREYHOUND — 100% Overload.
Approximately 3800 ft. coaster ride.
Time of ride approximately 2 minutes, 14 seconds.
4 trains to the ride, 3 coaches to a train.
Seating 18 people.
Sand test load 5400 lb.

BOOMERANG — 66⅔% Overload.
8 Tubs to the ride, seating 4 people to a tub.
Spin test 1000 lb. to a tub.
4 tubs released with normal load approximately
600 lb. sand test.

WATER BUG
Water Ride.
16 Tubs to the ride, 2 persons to a tub.
Tank 3½ feet deep, Size 56 feet x 66 feet.

ROCK-O-PLANE — 66⅔% Overload.
8 Cars, 2 Persons to a car.
Seating 16 people.
Sand load test 4000 lb., 5 bags to a car.

PAIR-O-CHUTES — Live Load.
6 parachutes to the ride, 2 people to a chute.
Approximately travels 180 feet high.
Test load approximately 500 lb. per chute.

ALADDIN'S CASTLE
Wooden Structure, Walk around fun devices.
10 fire exits.

Sandbags being loaded onto the Strat-O-Stat for the test load. 33⅓% overload 7200 lb.

These workmen are loading the Bobs train with sandbags, for the pre-testing load. 100% overload — 6600 lb.

The spring checkout being done by workmen.

Workmen shown coupling each 900 lb. unit or car together for spring testing.

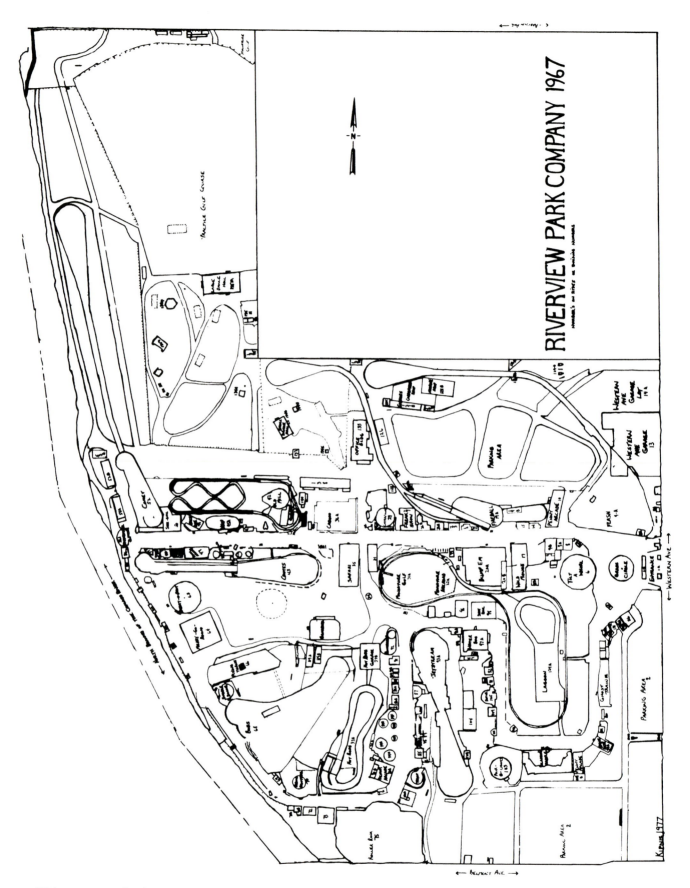

This map, made from an original blueprint, shows all the ride locations and attractions. You can match the numbers on the map with the numbers on the following pages for the small concessions and games. (L. Daunis — Photo by C. Wlodarczyk)

Do You Remember the Locations?

Refer to key for locations.

BUILDING NUMBER	BUILDING	YEAR BUILT	BOOTH NUMBER
76	Refreshment Stand	1940	9
77	Games Booth	1948	77
78	Games Booth	1940	58
79	Twist	1964	—
80-A-B	Penny Arcade and Toilets	1954-1955	Arcade #3
81	Games Booth	1938	39
82	Games Booth	1937	40-C
83	Ferris Wheel	1958	—
84-A-B-C-D-E-F	Kiddie City (Rodeo-Skyfighter-Fire Engine-Train-Tank-Games Booth-Carousel-Helicopter-Workshop)	1955-1951	—
85	Games Booth		4-A
86-A-B	Games Booth	1910-1957	43-44
87	Games Booth	1906	41
88-A-B	Games Booth	1910	46-47
90-A-B	Games Booth	1910	48A-48B
91	Games Booth	1910	49
92	Boomerang	1939	—
93-A-B	Jetstream	1965	—
94	Games Booth		Balloons
95	Games Booth	1943	50
96	Games Booth	1961	59
96-A	Games Booth	1909	52
97-A-B	Water Bug	1948-1952	—
98	Games Booth	1910-1955	53-19C
99	Refreshment Stand	1949	3
100	Games Booth	1937	53-C
101	Games Booth	1910	53-A
102	Refreshment Stand	1938	11
103	Pair-O-Chutes	1910-1936	—
104-A-B	Warehouse	1908-1955	—
105	Rotor	1952	—
106	1 Warehouse		—
107	Aladdins Castle	1932	—
108-A-B	Arcades & Toilets	1960	Arcade #4
109	Games Booth	1949	53-D
110	Photo Gallery	1910	55
111	Refreshment Stand	1948	12
112	Ghost Train	1928-1955	—
114	Rainbow Ice Stand	1945	17-B
115	Refreshment Stand	1946	1
116	Shooting Gallery	1906-1946	Gallery #3

117-A-B	Toilets and Area	1961	—
118	Bandshell	1910	—
119-A-B	General Toilets	1906	—
119-C	Incinerator	1961	—
120			—
121-A-B	Carnival Dressing Rooms		—
122			—
123	Paint Shop	1905	—
124-A-B	Lagoon and Warehouse	1957	—
125-A-B	Watchman Shanty	1910	—
126	Truscon Warehouse	1924	—
127-A-B-C	Auto Shop and Garages	1910	—
128-A-B-C	Carpenter & Machine Shop	1906-1955	—
129-A-B-C-D	Auto Parking #1 Gates	1925-40-55-58	—
130-A-B-C-D	Auto Parking #2 Gates	1940-1943	—
131-A	Rolloplane and Toilets	1951-1952	—
132	Baby Buggies	1951	57
133	Administration Bldg. Storerooms	1907	—
134-A to L	Small Picnic Grove	1906	—
135-A to R	Large Picnic Grove	1906	—
136-A to E	Golf Practice Course	1924	—
137	Warehouse	1910	—
138	Refreshment & Game Storerooms	1907	—
139			—
149	Ice House & Bottling Storerooms	1907	—
141	Warehouse	1910	—
142	Refreshment Stand	1910	6
143			—
144	Western Ave. Garage Lot	1907	—
146	Games Booth	1953	1
147	Games Booth	1951	60
148			—

The Names of the Rides

The following is a list of the rides with the name changes that had occurred during the years and also their approximate location in the park. In addition you will notice that the rides are broken down into the location or walkway on which they were located. Do you remember the park's layout in 1967? Maybe this will help you recall it:

Main Midway	*1967*
1. Tilt-A-Whirl	—Tilt-A-Whirl
2. Pippin, Silver Streak, Silver Flash	—Flash
3. Sky Rockets, Blue Streak	—Fireball
4. Twin Ferris Wheels	—The Wild Mouse
5. Dodgem	—Bump-em
6. Red Devil and Blue Devil Steam Engines	—Riverview Scout and Chief Diesel Locomotives
7. Caterpillar	—Caterpillar
8. Dancing Waters, Life Show	—Safari Ride
9. 1000 Islands, Mill on the Floss, Tunnel of Love (The Velvet Coaster once surrounded the 1000 Islands.)	—Old Mill
10. Shoot the Chutes	—Shoot the Chutes
11. Kiddyland #1	—Kiddyland #1
12. Whip	—Whip
13. Space Ride—West Station	—Space Ride—West Station
14. Cuddle Up	—Crazy Dazy
15. Big Dipper, Zephyr	—Comet
Riverwalk	
16. Hades Fun House	—Paratrooper
17. Aero-O-Stat	—Strat-O-Stat
18. Merry-Go-Round, Fairyland	—Merry-Go-Round
19. Kiddie Bobs	—Flying Turns
20. Indianapolis 500 Racers	—Bubble Bounce

21.	Bobs	—Bobs
22.	Jack Rabbit Racing Coaster	—Flying Scooter
23.	Moon Rocket	—Hot Rods

Bowery

24.	Ginger Snap, Virginia Reel, Krazy Ribbon	—Bingo Type Game after late 1940's called Stop N Shop
25.	Octopus, Flying Saucer, Mountain Road (area was originally covered by the Derby coaster)	—Twist
26.	Jitterbug Fun House, Fly-O-Planes, Flying Cars, Up and Over Cages, Calypso	—Big Ferris Wheel
27.	Kiddyland #2	—Kiddy City
28.	Boomerang	—Boomerang
29.	Greyhound	—Jet Stream

Chutes Walk

30.	Tumble Bug	—Water Bug
31.	Roll-O-Plane, Rock-O-Plane, Octopus	—Jet Rockets
32.	Rotor	—Rotor
33.	Eyeful Tower	—Pair-O-Chutes

Castle Walk

34.	Jack & Jill Slide, Figure 8, Cannon Ball Coaster, Bug House (burned down in early 1930's)	—Aladdin's Castle
35.	Ferris Wheels	—Space Ride-East Station
36.	Ophelia's Paradise, Spooktown	—Ghost Train
37.	Dive Bombers	—Roll-O-Plane

I've heard of the next few rides but I do not know where they were located in the park, maybe you do: Royal Gorge, Hey Day, Over the Falls, Derby Coaster, The Top (a roller coaster).

Also because the games, side shows and concessions were so numerous, I didn't include their names in this list, but I will mention a few of the different games.

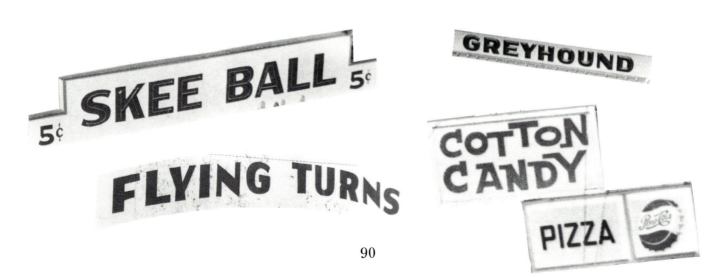

Operating Schedules

Riverview opened each year about the same time. The second Friday in May always started a season of fun and thrills for people of all ages. From Mid-May to Labor Day in September, millions entered the Main Gate on Western Avenue.

This mailer was sent out announcing the opening date for the 1967 season. (C. Wlodarczyk)

The busiest days each year were Memorial Day, 4th of July and Labor Day. You had to wait in line for every ride in the park on those days but it was always worth it.

The park was closed on Mondays with the exception of holidays falling on a Monday. Monday closing was instituted for about the last 15 years of the park's operations. Before that, Riverview was opened seven days a week. Each operating day opened at 11:30 A.M. and closed at Midnight. If a day was rainy or just slow due to weather, the barometer of the closing time was always the Bobs. The main gate would call the Bobs operator and see how the lines on the ride were. If the lines were long, the gate stayed open till closing. If the lines were short or thinning out the gate would close. The Bobs being the most popular ride in the park was really the accurate barometer in determining the size crowds for the day.

This is the back portion of the pass that was mailed to 3 or 4 million people, explaining the rules and regulations. (C. Wlodarczyk)

Recognize the front of the pass? Your name and address were typed on it. It told you of the discounts as well as the free admission to the park. (C. Wlodarczyk)

91

If you took your car to Riverview and decided to park in one of the parking lots, you would have to have 50¢ ready. For 10¢ to 15¢ you could enter the park, that is unless you had a free pass. Remember flashing that pass as if you were one of a select group to have received one. Little did you realize that 3 to 4 million were mailed out each season.

Riverview was famous for its 2¢ days and 5¢ nites. On these days and evenings the following rides were discounted: the Tilt-A-Whirl, Caterpillar, Miniature Trains, the Old Mill, Blue Streak, Comet and Greyhound. 2¢ Days were Mondays, Wednesdays and Fridays. 5¢ Nites were Tuesdays and Thursdays. In the latter years Mondays were dropped as discount days because the Park was closed on Mondays!

Riverview at the time of issuing these tickets for the final day of the last season, did not know it would be the last day forever! They had farewells other years also. (L. Daunis —Photo C. Wlodarczyk)

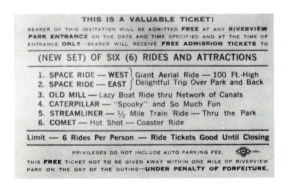

This is the back of the farewell ticket, it shows the free admission and the 6 free rides.
(L. Daunis — Photo C. Wlodarczyk)

92

1965 Riverview Courtesy Ticket and free ride coupons
(C. Wlodarczyk)

These were other free tickets
used on Special Days
(C. Wlodarczyk)

Special coupons used for free rides. (B. Reffke, R. Nichols —
Photo C. Wlodarczyk)

These coins or tokens were used before coupons were
used. (R. Garcia — Photo C. Wlodarczyk)

Riverview's Police Force had
Badges.
(R. Garcia—Photo C. Wlodarczyk)

These photos show the season passes that appeared in most papers in Chicago. (L. Daunis— Photo C. Wlodarczyk)

Employees had special passes, this one was for 1967 season.
(R. Garcia — Photo C. Wlodarczyk)

200,000 Pennies and Nickels Needed Daily

The rides used on 2¢ Days and 5¢ Nites were usually the same ones used on the special group tickets or used on special days.

To operate the park effectively, people and money were needed. In fact 75 to 80 year round employees worked at Riverview. During the operating season employees and concessionairs would number close to 900. About 190 men were used to operate the rides. Included in the 900 employees were: 17 carpenters, three electricians, a 27-man police force with many extras. Since Riverview had its own Fire Department and Fire Engine, naturally many men served as firemen.

I mentioned in addition to people, money was needed to help the park operate smoothly. This is some of the money needed to open each morning:

200,000 pennies and nickels

75,000 dimes

10,000 quarters

Riverview used so much small change in fact, that even large Chicago Banks had to send special orders to the U.S. Mint to help supply the needs of the park.

94

Special Group Outings

Riverview was always a popular place to enjoy a special day. Many companies would either rent the park for the day for just their employees and their families, or they would give their employees special discount tickets plus free passes for many of the rides. Many companies would sponsor picnics for their employees in addition to the rides. People could bring their picnic lunches and baskets and leave them in one of the picnic groves at Riverview and then spend the day enjoying themselves. Many of the special picnics and group outings were usually on the weekends. Following are some of the companies that had their special days at Riverview. Note some of the companies rented the park during special hours and the park was then closed to the public.

Crane Company — rental about $15,000.00 — Closed to Public
Electromotive Day — rental about $15,000.00 — Closed to Public
Motorola Company — rental about $15,000.00 — Closed to Public
9 A.M. to 5 P.M. on Saturday
United Charities — rental about $12,000.00 — On a Tuesday 5 P.M. till Midnight
(Riverview Rambles — United Charities paid the park and then all the proceeds went to the charities.)

Many of the following had special days:
Schwaben Day — 3 days originally Saturday, Sunday and Monday. Held in later part of August. There was always a Schwaben Pole decorated with fresh fruit and nuts during the harvest season.
Lineman's Local #9
Continental Can Day
Harmony Club #134
Ford Day
Schwinn Company
German, Bohemian, and
    Norwegian Days
Democratic Day

This poster appeared in stores promoting special days at Riverview. Customers were given tickets by retailer. (R. Garcia —Photo C. Wlodarczyk)

95

Special Tickets for Sponsored Days

Some of the special outings were sponsored by different food products. These companies had tickets printed and gave them to grocery stores to hand out. Maybe you picked some up at your local grocery store.

Each of these special tickets entitled you to free admission to the park and six free rides, the companies generally sponsoring this type of promotion were:

Coca Cola Day
Charlie Weber Day
Jay's Potato Chip Day
Certified Foods Day
   (Raggedy Ann Food Products)
Holsum Bread Day
Sinclair Gasoline Day

On the days that a certain company rented the park out for either the entire day or for a couple of hours, usually the employees could ride the rides as often as they desired, the only thing they paid for were the game booths and food. You may have some special memories of a day that you have spent at Riverview under these circumstances, I know I do.

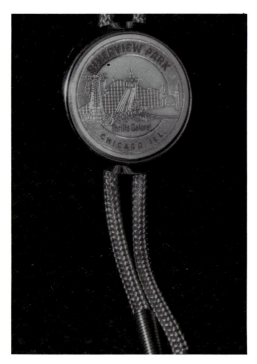

Rope tie with the Riverview Medallion could be purchased throughout the park. (R. Garcia — Photo C.Wlodarczyk)

Riverview Pennants (R. Garcia — Photo C. Wlodarczyk)

Insurance and Accident Rates

Riverview was actually much safer than most people really thought. The safety record of the park and also the fact that getting insurance coverage was no problem proves and supports this fact.

Lloyds of London and U.S. Fidelity and Guarantee covered the park for personal injuries, workman's compensation, of course, and liability. For an amusement park with the danger of accidents happening frequently you would think that Riverview would pay an extremely high insurance premium, but in actuality according to the park's accountant the premium was around $100,000.00 per year.

EXCELLENT SAFETY RECORD FOR 64 YEARS

The excellent safety record for Riverview shows in the accident rates. In 1935 the accident rate was 4.35 per 100,000 and then in 1960 the rate was as low as .007 per 100,000 people. As far as amusement parks go these were very low rates.

Only 6 people lost their lives at Riverview during the 64 year history of the park. Only 2 of the 6 deaths were due to the park's fault. These occurred on the Aero-o-stat (more commonly known to us as the Strat-O-Stat in recent years). The cables broke on the ride and the plane flew into the Chicago River and it was then that two people were said to have drowned. One man was killed on the Bobs when he is reported to have stood up on a 25 foot banked curve and then flew out on to the tracks where he was run over by the next train. On the other famous roller coaster, the Fireball, the same kind of accident happened, a man stood up so that he could wave to friends and in doing so was killed.

A SENSELESS DEATH BECAUSE OF CARELESSNESS

Another senseless accident happened on the Flying Cars located on the Bowery for only one or two years at that time. The cars on this ride went around in a barrel and the rider could step on the brake in the car and it would go upside down with the rolling barrel. In this accident the young girl failed to fasten her safety belt as she had been warned to. The final death was on the old Mill on the Floss ride. This was a ride operator who lost his life. He was getting ready to jump over canal to go to one of the islands of this ride (this was done regularly because lovers got off the boats so the men would check from time to time). As he stepped off he slipped into the canal and was crushed by an approaching boat and then later by the paddle wheel that moved the flow of the water. Truly the four deaths mentioned here could have been prevented if the people involved had only stopped to think about the consequences of carelessness. What a shame and pity for people to die senselessly.

There were minor accidents and injuries in the park over the years but the one that happened in 1937 on the Pippin was considered to be about the worst. The Pippin roller coaster (the Silver Flash in later years) had trains running and somehow a train uncoupled and rolled back into a low valley of a hill till the next train ran into it. About 60 or 70 people were injured, but no deaths occurred.

In spite of the sore backs, necks and bruises, the safety record was really good. Riverviews rides were inspected daily. If a ride would malfunction during the day, it was corrected immediately (unlike many of the parks operating now, closing rides for the season for repairs). The reason was that to Riverview a downed ride meant loss of revenue. So two reasons rides were kept in top notch shape and functioning properly—one for safety, two for revenue.

Power failures did happen occasionally, one such time was on the Silver Flash. In 1952 during a power failure the train came to a stop on top of the first hill. People were forced to walk down the wooden structure with the help of park employees. All of the roller coasters had built in steps on the hills, so that in case of emergencies such as this one, (caused by Commonwealth Edison) you could get down safely.

Mr. Schmidt, the owner, had a habit of always going on the new rides first and also ride the park's rides early in the spring before the public started coming. Another safety factor: If he tested and passed them, people probably felt more comfortable about riding them.

Miscellaneous Information About Riverview

THE MARDI GRAS PARADE

The last three weeks of Riverview's season was reserved for the Carnival or Mardi Gras Parade. Each evening during the Mardi Gras, kids that came in costumes were given free admission to the park and also free rides. Then the thrill of it all: they could march around with the parade which was composed of many bands and floats. It all started every night at 8:30 P.M.

Many of the bands that took their turns in the parades over the years were: Elks All City Youth Band—Kenosha, Wisconsin; Lake Band—Milwaukee, Wisconsin; Racine Boy Scouts Drum and Bugle Corps—Racine, Wisconsin; Racine Kilties—Racine, Wisconsin; La Porte High School—La Porte, Indiana; St. Rita High School—Chicago, Illinois; Joliet High School—Joliet, Illinois; 175 piece band from Indianapolis, Indiana; Watervliet High School—Watervliet, Michigan; Holland, Michigan, High School Band; etc.

These are just a few of the bands that marched, spaced between the Mardi Gras Floats in the parade each year. Were you in one of those bands?

From the early 1930's through the late 1940's there was no Carnival or Mardi Gras because of the fire that had burned down the Bug House. The reason was that all the floats used in the parades were stored there during the off season and they were destroyed along with the Bug House.

THE FREAK SHOW

Do you remember the Palace of Wonders, Congress of Oddities or, as we all remember it, the Freak Show? It had quite a variety, the Rubber Man, the Sword Swallower, the Smallest Mother and Daughter in the world, the Tallest Man, the Fat Boy, the Fat Woman, the Snake Charmer, the Man with no legs, the Two-Faced Boy, the Tattooed Lady, Pop-Eye, Belly Dancers, Midgets . . . and the list went on and on. It was said that the Freak Show at Riverview was bigger than the one at Ringling Brothers Circus.

The #3 Bobs train whipping around the low front curve. (C. Wlodarczyk)

SPRING CLEANUP WAS COSTLY

In the spring of each of the 64 years, that is, around March 1st, it was time to get the park in shape for the coming season. All the rides were load tested, every ride that needed painting received a fresh coat. Speaking of paint, 6,000 gallons were used each year. In fact, 150,000 board feet of lumber was used, 30,607 light bulbs for the 52 banjo lights and main entrance were used in the spring not counting the replacement bulbs used throughout the season.

Additionally, thousands of feet of neon tubing and spot and flood lights going in wattage from 10 to 10,000 watts were used. 1,500,000 gallons of water were used to fill the Chutes pond, the Tunnel of Love and other water rides and the concessions. Riverview had four shooting galleries so each season 3,500,000 rounds of ammunition were used.

In the fall of each year after the park had closed, a protective rustoleum grease coating was put on the tracks of the roller coasters. In the spring this coating had to be scraped off and a new grease was put on the tracks and also the wheels of the coasters. All the roller coasters had automatic braking systems for safety.

Do You Remember?

Do you remember **the Beer** Garden when it was called the Palm Gardens?

Do you remember **that** Russ Young was the organist at the Roller Rink?

Do you remember the penny arcade machines with post cards? Each season **1,750,000** postcards of movie stars and park scenes were sold.

MISCELLANEOUS INFORMATION

Do you remember the days of Big Bill Thompson? The car fare was paid to and from the park with bright new shiny pennies. Right inside the Main Gate kids would take their pennies from a big table.

Do you remember how high the Pair-O-Chutes were? The structure was 212 feet high, but sitting in the seat you would only go up about 187 feet.

Do you remember what happened in 1939 on the Pair-O-Chutes? A Couple got married on the Pair-O-Chutes that year.

Do you remember how much food was used at the park every year? Food was always important to your visit to the park so 60,000 ice cream cones, 40 tons of popcorn, 1 million bags, ½ million hot dogs, 250,000 candy bars, 1,500,000 cups and 750,000 napkins were ordered each year. (But no straws)

TWO TON BAKER

Do you remember Two Ton Baker? His laugh made you remember the slogan for Riverview "laugh your troubles away." Interestingly every season for several years the commercials on television showed him riding the rides at Riverview, but really he never did ride any of them. For example, they showed him riding the Bobs, or so it seemed, actually he was seated in the car and pushed around the low curve, then the film was sped up to make it look like he was really riding.

The same for whatever rides he was pictured on. When the Wild Mouse was installed, he got in one of the cars and was pushed to one of the hills, because of his weight the tracks gave way beneath him and there he hung suspended in air. Of course these tracks were safe, but at the time of the shooting of the commercial the construction of the Mouse was not completed, so a temporary structure was supported by 2 x 4's haphazardly for the shooting. Two Ton Baker was Riverview's good will ambassador.

THREE TRAINS ON THE "BOBS"

On the Bobs with all three trains running, the brakes were essential as the trains ran about 50 seconds apart, so you see timing was important. The second ride fare was received when the train pulled into the station but if someone was slow about getting their change out, they were either ordered out or given a free ride, since there was no time to dilly dally. If the train was loaded with 2nd riders sometimes all 2nd ride fares could not be collected. That train was called a Flyer—meaning someone was riding again without paying because all the fares could not be collected in that short time. Did you ever wonder what kept the operators honest with the second ride fares? There were always back up people watching them to make sure they collected and accounted for the money. Fare collectors would yell out Flyer, if all fares were not collected, to the back up people and they would account for the Free-Bees in their cash reports.

The Bobs train was very heavy, with each seat weighing 900 pounds making the total train without riders close to 10,000 pounds. It was the flanged railroad type wheels that gave the Bobs its roughness and bounce. The Bobs averaged 7 to 8 million riders per year for first rides and close to 300,000 second riders. Did you ride again? The speed was 65 mph on the Bobs and the height of the first hill was about 85 feet. Wow, what a ride!

When winds were gusty as they were the day this picture was taken, the Pair-O-Chutes did not operate. Safety Standards were always met. (C. Wlodarczyk)

101

Carl Jeske, the manager of the Bobs had one of the largest earring collections in the world. What was unique was that not one earring matched up with another, because of this Mr. Jeske's collection was written up in Ripley's *Believe It or Not*. If you have an odd earring laying around the house the mate is probably still in Mr. Jeske's collection.

So spring meant work for Riverview employees, all the rides had to be taken out of storage and put together, they had to be checked for safety. New rides were installed and old ones taken down and stored. They were stored due to some insurance procedure, for example the Blue Streak and Greyhound trains were still on the property at the park's closing. Many of the rides or part of the rides were built right there on the premises.

Look at all the terror-stricken faces on the people as the Fireball shoots down its first hill.
(C. Wlodarczyk)

Wide angle view taken
from the Space Ride,
note assorted rides.
(J. Kolberg)

Notice the boat on top of the Chutes Tower, the Tumble Bug in foreground in Kiddyland and the Strat-O-Stat in background. (C. Wlodarczyk)

Chutes Pond and boat taken from the Space Ride. A good view of Riverview's Picnic Grove. Note the back of the Bobs in the upper right hand corner. (J. Kolberg)

The Chutes, Kiddyland, Space Ride, Paratrooper and Comet roller Coaster. (C. Wlodarczyk)

Remember getting wet like these riders on the Chutes? The Old Tunnel of Love is in the background.
(C. Wlodarczyk)

The Greyhound roller coaster, Boomerang, Space Ride and Pair-O-Chutes Tower. (J. Kolberg)

This view of the Greyhound's
trackage shows how long
the ride was, but also how mild.
(C. Wlodarczyk)

Aladdin's Castle as seen from the Space Ride. (C. Wlodarczyk)

107

Remember riding the Riverview Chief on 2¢ days or 5¢ nites as the sign shows located just above the engine. (C. Wlodarczyk)

Maybe you were one of the riders on the Riverview Scout as it slipped past Aladdin's Castle. (C. Wlodarczyk)

The sign on Western Avenue announcing the opening date of 1968 which never became a reality.
(J. Luka)

The Derby roller coaster at Riverview. (the date and photographer unknown)

Aladdin's eyes are stilled for the last time during the winter of 1967.
(J. Kolberg from collection of K. Reiger)

Everything around Aladdin is gone, the Castle was next. Aladdin's Castle was one of the last to go.
(J. Kolberg from the collection of K. Reiger)

Main entrance as it looked from Western Avenue.
(Photo reprinted by permission of the *Chicago Sun-Times*)

Jack Rabbit racing coaster during the 1920's. Note the ornate wood working on the front of the structure.

Flying Turns train twisting thru the curves.

112

Another view of the popular Flying Turns ride at Riverview.

War of the Worlds attraction of the 1920's. (F. Fournier)

Old view of magnificent Merry-Go-Round at Riverview.
(Photo reprinted by permission of the *Chicago Sun-Times*)

A 1940's view of this popular attraction at Riverview with its stunt riders.

This early view shows the Merry-Go-Round building, the Aero-Stat tower and a maze of coaster tracks. Pre-Bob's era. (Photo reprinted by permission of the
Chicago Sun-Times)

Shoot the Chutes tower and slide with the pond drained. Note the Devil's head used on the tunnel entrance back then. (Photo reprinted by permission of the
Chicago Sun-Times)

115

Aerial view of the Bowery area with the brand new Jetstream coaster built in 1965 to replace the popular but old Greyhound coaster. (Photo reprinted by permission of the *Chicago Sun-Times*)

The old Bughouse at nite was the most popular funhouse at Riverview until it burned down in the early 30's. (F. Fournier)

Early photo of Mill on the Floss Ride. Note: Two boats in the canals.
(Photo reprinted by permission of the *Chicago Sun-Times*)

Fireball train drops down that first steep hill, distorting faces and leaving all gasping for air. (C. Wlodarczyk)

This was the show inside the Motorcycle Syndrome. Daring acts done with great skill. (Photo reprinted by permission of the *Chicago Sun-Times*)

The Virginia Reel later called the Crazy Ribbon goes up the chainlift. This ride operated next to the Roller Rink thru 1948. To see the ride layout turn to page 51. (F. Fournier)

Bobs train #2 slams into the front banked curve. Note how the people are thrown to one side and no hands up!!! (Photo reprinted by permission of the *Chicago Sun-Times*)

This 1929 aerial view showing Riverview's 8 coasters, count them! A few years later the Flying Turns were re-constructed and then there were 9. (Photo reprinted by permission of the *Chicago Sun-Times*)

The back curves of the Bobs from the top of the first hill. Note how sharply banked those spaghetti bowl turns were. What a ride! Who wants to ride again? I do! (F. Fournier)

Comments on other Amusement Parks

Ratings: 1 star fair, 2 stars good, 3 stars quite good, 4 stars excellent

No matter where we may go, from East coast to West coast, we'll never find an amusement park or a theme park that can compare with Riverview. There are several reasons. First of all, you'll never come across a park that has 6 roller coasters plus the rides that Riverview had. You also won't find many parks that have a reasonable price for general admission like that at Riverview. I haven't been in a park where there is a second ride policy like the one Riverview had. Also at most parks with roller coasters of some type you do not have the choice of waiting for the last seat like you did at Riverview. I've waited sometimes for 30 minutes to ride in the last seat of the Bobs, once in I could usually stay there as long as I wished or until the cash ran out. I rode the Bobs some 10 or 15 times in a row on some visits to the park. The newer parks do not generally allow second rides unless you get off and stand in line again to get on. The more popular the ride the longer the wait. Some lines have two and three hour waits for a ride on the roller coasters.

Since Riverview is gone and we can no longer "laugh our troubles away" as Two-Ton Baker would have said, let's review some of the parks around the country, starting close to home.

The Turn of the Century at Great America, Gurnee, Illinois. This view shows this coaster's biggest drop. (C. Wlodarczyk)

The corkscrew on the Turn of the Century similar to other steel coasters in other amusement parks. (C. Wlodarczyk)

SIX FLAGS GREAT AMERICA, Gurnee, Illinois - The year 1984 showed great promise for Great America, ownership changed hands from the Mariott Corporation to Bally-Six Flags Management. In the past all the other Six Flags Parks were superior to Great America as far as rides, park layout and attractions go. But now with Six Flags putting money into new rides and attractions, the potential for Gurnee, Illinois to have the premier Six Flags Amusement Park is a reality. Major rides include 2 water flume rides, new water raft rapids ride, The American Eagle a twin racing coaster (the world's highest roller coaster - 147 feet 10 inches tall), The Demon corkscrew-looping coaster built by Arrow Development and Willard's Wizard a steel coaster, also a tri-wheel ferris wheel type ride. Wouldn't it be great if Great America had a theme area called "Riverview" or how terrific to have the World Famous Bobs rebuilt??? Interstate 294 at Exist 132. (312) 249-1776★★★

121

AMERICANA AMUSEMENT PARK, Middletown, Ohio — The home of "The Screechin' Eagle" a wooden roller coaster. Located about 30 miles from Kings Island. It's an old-fashioned park with rides such as The Paratrooper, Octopus, Flying Scooters, Calypso, Tilt-A-Whirl, Rock-O-Plane and paddle boats just to name a few. The park contains a lake within its boundaries and is well kept and run well. 5757 Middletown-Hamilton Rd. 45042. (512) 539-7339★★

DORNEY PARK, Allentown Pennsylvania — One of the top 10 coasters in the U.S. A wild woodie that moves "Coaster" really makes you hang on during the ride. The park has a cuddle up type ride housed indoors called the Iceburg. Also a pirate swing ship, an old mill ride, a strat-o-stat airplane ride, The Flying Dutchman a steel coaster, a good fun house called Bucket of Blood and other rides and attractions. Park is well run and clean, the ducks in the pond are beggars! Dorney lost a magnificent carousel this last winter due to a fire. Take my word for it Dorney Park is worth the trip if your near that area, stop and visit a great park and a ride a great coaster. 3830 Dorney Park Rd. 18104. (215) 395-3724★★★

Photo to left shows Screeching Eagle. Top photo shows trackage of same coaster. Notice ground level dips.
(C. Wlodarczyk)

122

SIX FLAGS OVER MID AMERICA, Eureka, Missouri. Just west of St. Louis. This is a great theme park, with a great wooden roller coaster called the Screamin' Eagle. This coaster is one of the best I have ridden since the Bobs, it is fast, somewhat rough and has some good drops. (See the facts sheet; it includes interesting information.) Other rides include a Water Flume ride, Bumpem Cars, Rotor and an old Carousel built in 1915 (still in beautiful shape). For a while the Screamin' Eagle holds the world's record as the longest, tallest and fastest roller coaster. As good as the Screamin' Eagle is, I still think the Bobs were greater and I know much rougher. ★★★★

SIX FLAGS®
OVER MID-AMERICA
Box 666, Eureka, Missouri 63025
Bob Kochan, Public Relations Manager

ROLLER COASTER FACT SHEET

NAME	The Screamin' Eagle
OPENING DATE	April 10, 1976
TRACK LENGTH	3,872 LF
HORIZONTAL LENGTH	3,592 LF
HEIGHT	110 LF
SPEED	62 MPH
MAXIMUM DROPS	92' 87'
NUMBER OF FOOTINGS	1,278
CUBIC YARDS OF CONCRETE	886
BOARD FEET OF LUMBER	550,000
NUMBER OF MAN HOURS	130,000
GALLONS OF PAINT	10,000
POUNDS OF BOLTS	50,000
POUNDS OF NAILS	15,400
DESIGNER	John Allen of Philadelphia
STRUCTURAL ENGINEER	Bill Cobb of Dallas
CONSULTANT	Don Rosser of Atlanta
GENERAL CONTRACTOR	W. Norm Howells, Jr. President, Frontier Construction Company

The trackage of the Screamin' Eagle at Six Flags in St. Louis, Missouri, from the top of the incline looks impressive and is. It is the world's largest, highest and fastest. (C. Wlodarczyk)

123

15 cars of the Screamin' Eagle plunge
down the first hill of 87 feet. The third hill
is even higher, 92 feet. (C. Wlodarczyk)

The 3rd hill of the Screamin' Eagle, notice
how steep as the train starts its trip down.
(C. Wlodarczyk)

KINGS ISLAND, Kings Mill, Ohio—Just north
of Cincinnati. This is another great theme park
that seems to have a soft spot for the old
amusement park that was once in Cincinnati,
Coney Island. This park installed one section
called Coney Island. They built a wooden Twin
Racing Coaster a few years ago. It is a great
coaster ride. The Red Racer and the Blue Racer
do just what their names imply, they race. The
winner always being the train that has the most
weight in it.

The Racer was built by the Philadelphia
Toboggan Company.

Capacity on the Racer—1 Hour with 4 trains
running—3000 people

Capacity on the Racer—1 Hour with 2 trains
running—1440 people

Top Speed—61 MPH

Length of Tracks—6830 feet or 1.29 miles

Height of the first hill—88 feet

The Fountains and gift shop area
of Kings Island, Kings Mill, Ohio.
(C. Wlodarczyk)

124

In its Coney Island section, Kings Island has a Flying Scooter ride, a Tumble Bug, Cuddle Up and Bumpem Cars as well as many other rides.★★★

Kings Island Blue Racer starts out.
(C. Wlodarczyk)

Kings Island Red Racer rounds the curve.
(C. Wlodarczyk)

Riding the Racer looks something like this.
(C. Wlodarczyk)

Down the Racers plunge 88 feet, still racing up and down all the other hills.
(C. Wlodarczyk)

MAGIC MOUNTAIN, Valencia, California—35 miles North of Los Angeles. A gigantic park with many, many rides, including a steel Roller Coaster called the Revolution. It is different from other steel coasters in that it does not go through a cork screw loop but rather it does make a 360 degree revolution at a fast speed. I'm really hung up on wooden coasters, but in my estimation this is the best steel coaster I have ever been on. If you are ever on the West Coast, make sure you stop here. Really about all the park needs is a good old fashion wooden roller coaster.★★★

BELMONT PARK, San Diego, California—This park had a wooden Roller Coaster called the Earthquake. It was a fast, rough ride. I'm using the past tense since the park is closed and all the rides with the exception of the coaster will go. The roller coaster is supposed to stay and operate again in the future. I surely hope so, since I rode the Earthquake a few years ago and really thought it was a fast, rough ride. The coaster rated four stars; the park was average.

The Earthquake roller coaster, Belmont Park, San Diego, California, was a rough coaster. I hope they save it. (J. Templin)

Look at the Earthquake's trackage, its curves and banked track remind me so much of the Bobs. (J. Templin)

Cedar Point, Sandusky, Ohio is the home of the Blue Streak zipping down the first hill. (N. Oyen)

A good wooden roller coaster, the Blue Streak is at Cedar Point, Sandusky, Ohio. (C. Wlodarczyk)

The mighty Thunderbolt at Kennywood Park, Pittsburgh. The #2 rated coaster, a great ride, fast, steep and great curves. (C. Wlodarczyk)

The Cyclone at Lakeside Park, Denver, Colorado is a favorite park and a favorite coaster of mine. Lots of trackage and terrific drops and curves. (C. Wlodarczyk)

The Blue Streak's first drop at Cedar Point. A very fast out and backer with some great drops along the way. (C. Wlodarczyk)

127

Water flume at Knotts Berry Farm, Buena Park, California is the best overall flume ride in the country. (C. Wlodarczyk)

Back curves and tunnel on the Thunderbolt at Kennywood Park. Note how the coaster is built in and out of valleys. Super ride! (C. Wlodarczyk)

The Wildcat at Idora Park, Youngstown, Ohio. #8 coaster before the fire destroyed the back portion of this coaster. We all hope the park rebuilds that section and keeps this great coaster rolling and in the top ten! (C. Wlodarczyk)

The Tornado rolls near the corn fields in central Iowa. An above average coaster with good drops and curves A fast out and backer on one of those hot Iowa days at Adventureland, Des Moines, Iowa. (C. Wlodarczyk)

Giant Dipper at Santa Cruz, California. Super ride fast great fan curves. #9 nationally you board the Dipper on the inside loading platform. The Giant Dipper runs rain or shine! (C. Wlodarczyk)

#1 coaster the Texas Cyclone, Astroworld, Houston, TX. Its rough, its fast and its almost another Bobs. If you ever get down to Texas do not miss a ride on the Daddy of all operating coasters!! (M. Meyer)

The Dorney Park Coaster rated #10 is a combination out and backer, twister, great drops, curves and tunnel but still maintains a good pace thru-out the ride. (C. Wlodarczyk)

The awesome Colossus opened in 1977 at Six Flags Magic Mountain near Los Angeles, CA. Good Drops, lots of trackage on this twin racer. (C. Wlodarczyk)

Front section of Kennywood's Thunderbolt. Note the loading platform on the left. What a start to a ride, a 70 ft. drop into a gully right out of the loading platform. (C. Wlodarczyk)

The Great American Scream Machine at Six Flags over Georgia. A great out and backer with good steep drops. One of the most beautiful coasters anywhere. (C. Wlodarczyk)

The Comet, Hershey Park, Hershey, PA.
Great coaster, the first drop is right over the river that winds thru the park. Great park to visit and don't miss the chocolate tour. (C. Wlodarczyk)

Circus World's Roaring Tiger. A good out and backer, its fast, smooth and steep. Close to Disney world and Epcot, don't miss it. (C. Wlodarczyk)

131

The Beast at Kings Island. This one will bring you to your knees. It's steep, very fast with tunnels, 2 lift chains and a helix of 540° you wish you could by-pass. WOW! (C. Wlodarcyzk)

The Great American Revolution, Magic Mountain. A super steel coaster that has one 360° loop. The first of its kind with a lot of trackage, good drops, curves and about all you can ask for. Used in movies and on T.V. shows since its construction. (C. Wlodarczyk)

Entrance to Dorney Park, Allentown,
Pennsylvania. A good old fashioned amusement
park, well run with a lot of rides. (C. Wlodarczyk)

Great American Scream Machine at
Six Flags Over Georgia out of
the back seat down the 1st hill over
the lake. Great ride, great park.
(C. Wlodarczyk)

Kennywood Racer in the background. The log flume in
the foreground. The Racer is an excellent smaller coaster,
trains switch positions in the station on every trip.
How is this done? I know! (C. Wlodarczyk)

The American Eagle, Six Flags Great
America, Gurnee, IL. It's the best
initial first hill drop I've been down.
147 ft. 10 in. (C. Wlodarczyk)

My Favorite Amusement Theme Parks

CEDARPOINT, Sandusky, Ohio - Cedarpoint's motto is "The Amazement Park" and that it is. Surrounded by bodies of water, Lake Erie on one side and Sandusky Bay on the other. A giant park with great rides, great coasters, has hotel and campground on property, also a boat marina. Cedarpoint has something for everyone, I really do not call it a theme park but its run on the theme park operation procedure. But if it's a theme park or and amusement park - who cares - it's #1.

KINGS ISLAND, Kings Mill, Ohio (near Cincinnati) - This is a great park, more than plenty of rides, shows and attractions are the best. Kings Island is the home of 2 great coasters, as well as a great management group.

SIX FLAGS OVER GEORGIA (near Atlanta, Georgia) - Six Flags has six themed areas with over 100 different rides, shows and adventures. The Great American Scream Machine is a roller coaster thriller. Six Flags is also the home of the beautiful "RIVERVIEW" carousel. It is the park's fine china and one of the most beautiful carousels in the world.

SIX FLAGS - MAGIC MOUNTAIN, Valencia, California (near Los Angeles) - A big, big park increasing its size by over 50% since its opening. Magic Mountain's roller coasters are movie stars seen in the movies Rollercoaster and National Lampoon's Vacation. A class park with great shows.

KNOTTSBERRY FARM, Buena Park, California - This park is one that all ages will really enjoy from the rides to the restaurants (the chicken is super) to the extensive gift shops. When in California don't miss Knotts Berry Farm.

SIX FLAGS OVER MID AMERICA, Eureaka, Missouri (near St. Louis) - Home of a top coaster "The Screamin' Eagle". The park is situated in a hilly area which makes the park even more beautiful. The shows are good and worth seeing. The quality of operation and management really contribute to a great park.

ASTROWORLD, Houston Texas - Home of a massive traditional coaster ranked #1 the Texas Cyclone. Astroworld was the first park to have a water rapids ride. The park has over 100 rides and attractions.

ADVENTURELAND, Des Moines, Iowa - A smaller theme park out in the middle Iowa just off Interstate 80. It is small in size but mighty in entertainment. Great rides and the layout of the park makes sure you do not miss any of them. Tornado is what they call their roller coaster and it alone is worth a trip to Iowa. The lines for the rides are not nearly as long as some of the bigger major theme parks so you can get a lot of coaster riding in.

HERSHEY PARK, Hershey, Pennsylvania — If you are a chocoholic this is the place for you. Before entering the park you'll be fascinated by the sweet pungent smell of chocolate coming from downtown Hershey. Street lights in the shape of Candy Kisses line the way to Chocolate World which you tour first before entering the park. Then take a scenic ride on the 330 ft. Kissing Tower. Then be sure and ride one of the country's best coasters the Comet. Don't miss the Sooperdooperlooper.

CIRCUS WORLD, Haines City, Florida - Only 10 miles west of Walt Disney World. The circus theme is employed throughout the park as distinguished by the huge Big Top you will see as you approach the park. If you look carefully you'll be able to see and touch the south's fearsome Roaring Tiger. The Roaring Tiger is the highest coaster in the south and is a good and fast out and backer.

Walt Disney, a creative genius gave us two entertainment complexes that are truly more than just amusement parks. Disneyland and Walt Disney World are unique in themselves and definitely have an aura different than the parks I've previously mentioned. Both are billed as Magic Kingdoms and they are, giving credit where credit is due.

Nothing will replace Riverview in our memories, but if on vacation and you are looking for something to do, ride a roller coaster and if you find one as terrifying as the Bobs, let me know!

My Favorite Traditional Amusement Parks

KENNYWOOD PARK, West Mifflin, Pennsylvania (suburb of Pittsburgh) - This one rates high on everyone's list of good old fashioned parks. Kennywood has plenty of rides (more than 32 major rides) and 4 wooden roller coasters, 2 are rated nationally in the top 15 coasters. Don't forget to try the french fries!!!!★★★★

LAKESIDE PARK, Denver, Colorado - This park is old but well maintained. Some of the good old rides found at Lakeside are not found at all parks. The coaster "Cyclone" is in my top 15. In the evening when you take the train around the lake you see the beauty of the park and its tower near the main gate shining brightly from all the neon lights. The Fun House is the best one I've visited and you can enjoy the fun house as long as you wish. Take a stroll down to the lake and feed popcorn to the carp and watch the ducks walk over the fish to get the popcorn.★★★★

DORNEY PARK, Allentown, Pennsylvania - The coaster is rated in everyone's top 10. The park has over 50 rides and attractions. Uniquely a road goes right thru the center of the park with a crossing guard making sure no one gets hurt on their day of fun.★★★★

IDORA PARK, Youngstown, Ohio - Nice traditional park with plenty of rides and a beautiful Merry-Go-Round. The roller coaster "The Wildcat" is in the top ten coasters and will remain there providing the park rebuilds the portion lost to a fire this past winter.★★★★

ELITCH'S GARDENS, Denver, Colorado - Mr. Twister, an excellent coaster rates #2 or #3 on most coaster fan's list. The park looks like a large garden with rides and attractions added to enhance the gardens which they do. Elitch's is beautiful and known for its garden arrangements.★★★★

SANTA CRUZ BEACH BOARDWALK, Santa Cruz, California - This park offers old fashioned family fun, it has rides, games, shows and a mile-long beach. Great park with a top 10 woodie coaster on the ocean. The coaster is a twister and is well maintained.★★★★

LAGOON PARK, Farmington, Utah (near Salt Lake City) - Lagoon has good rides and a good coaster. It is well maintained and has a first class playhouse.★★★★

AMERICANA AMUSEMENT PARK, Middletown, Ohio - Approximately 20-30 miles from Kings Island, great park with plenty of the traditional type rides. Americana's coaster is not super high but has plenty of ground level steep drops and it really moves.★★★★

BELL'S AMUSEMENT PARK, Tulsa, Oklahoma - Bell's is a family owned park and is well maintained. A unique brick carpeted midway adds to the park's beauty. Zingo, the roller coaster, makes a trip to the park worthwhile. Stop by and say "hi" to Mr. Bell.★★★★

GEAUGA LAKE PARK, Aurora, Ohio - Situated picturesquely on a lake across from Sea World. The park has over 100 rides, shows and attractions. The Big Dipper coaster takes you on 2 minutes 30 seconds of thrills.★★★★

EPILOGUE

Riverview is gone, but not forgotten. In the spring of 1967 it opened for what was to be its last season. It closed its gates, as always, on Labor Day evening, supposedly to open again in May, 1968, for its 65th season. In fact, the license had been purchased that fall for the 65th season and also the new sign had been painted and put up showing the opening date in 1968.

Much speculation has been said about why the park closed, that is all it is, speculation. No one knows for sure. Some feel that racial problems closed the park, some say that the stockholders were offered a good deal and didn't want to pass it up. Whatever the reason, Riverview was sold to the dismay and sadness of millions. The park was sold for approximately 6½ million dollars on October 3, 1967, and never reopened. Interestingly enough today that 6½ million dollars could not even rebuild the Bobs.

Whatever reasons are given for the destruction of an era, the over 200 million visitors to Riverview Park will never forget the good times they enjoyed there. Memories can never be sold! Aren't we glad? I hope through the pages of this book, through the words and photographs, your memories were rekindled. I know mine were in the compiling of information and history.

Riverview is gone, but is not forgotten . . .

Chuck Wlodarczyk